Global Risks and International Law

Developments in International Law

VOLUME 79

The titles published in this series are listed at *brill.com/diil*

Global Risks and International Law

The Case of Climate Change and Pandemics

By

Sarah Cassella

BRILL | NIJHOFF

LEIDEN | BOSTON

Library of Congress Cataloging-in-Publication Data

Names: Cassella, Sarah, author.
Title: Global risks and international law : the case of climate change and pandemics / by Sarah Cassella.
Description: Leiden ; Boston : Brill/Nijhoff, 2024. | Series: Developments in international law, 0924-5332 ; volume 79 | Includes bibliographical references and index. | Contents: International legal concept of global risk – The role of international law in dealing with global risks – Responsibilities for global risks – Looking forward, the paths of solidarity. |
Identifiers: LCCN 2023045647 (print) | LCCN 2023045648 (ebook) | ISBN 9789004538696 (hardback) | ISBN 9789004538702 (ebook)
Subjects: LCSH: International law. | Environmental law, International. | Climatic changes–Law and legislation. | Pandemics.
Classification: LCC KZ3410 .C39 2024 (print) | LCC KZ3410 (ebook) | DDC 344.04/3–dc23/eng/20231003
LC record available at https://lccn.loc.gov/2023045647
LC ebook record available at https://lccn.loc.gov/2023045648

Typeface for the Latin, Greek, and Cyrillic scripts: "Brill". See and download: brill.com/brill-typeface.

ISSN 0924-5332
ISBN 978-90-04-53869-6 (hardback)
ISBN 978-90-04-53870-2 (e-book)
DOI 10.1163/9789004538702

This book is printed on acid-free paper and produced in a sustainable manner.

Contents

Acknowledgments

This book is the outcome of a research project begun in 2019 that has been slightly delayed by the COVID-19 pandemic which, unfortunately, gave me much material to work on.

It would not have been possible to write it without the support of several institutions. In particular, in 2021–2022 I was granted a sabbatical in order to work on it by the French *Conseil national des Universités* and by the University of Le Mans. I also had the opportunity to make much progress on it in October 2021 as a visiting scholar at the Max Planck Institute for Comparative Public Law and International Law in Heidelberg, where I had the chance to talk to several researchers. I would particularly like to thank Anne Peters for her hospitality and for our fruitful discussions on the topic.

A final word of thanks goes to the students and colleagues at the University Paris Cité whose comments on the subject of my work helped me to further my thinking; special thanks in this regard go to my colleague and friend Anne-Thida Norodom, an expert in cyber risks with whom I hope to continue to work on this fascinating topic.

Abbreviations

AJIL	American Journal of International Law
ARIO	Articles on Responsibility of International Organisations
ARSIWA	Articles on Responsibility of States for Internationally Wrongful Acts
BIT	Bilateral investment treaty
CEDAW	Convention on the Elimination of All Forms of Discrimination Against Women
CESCR	Committee on Economic, Social and Cultural Rights
CETA	EU-Canada Comprehensive Economic and Trade Agreement
CRC	Committee on the Rights of the Child
CUP	Cambridge University Press
ECJ	European Court of Justice
ECtHR	European Court of Human Rights
EJIL	European Journal of International Law
ESIL	European Society of International Law
EU	European Union
GATT	General Agreement on Tariffs and Trade
GHG	Greenhouse Gas
IACHR	Interamerican Court of Human Rights
ICAO	International Civil Aviation Organisation
ICCPR	International Covenant on Civils and Political Rights
ICJ	International Court of Justice
IHR	International Health Regulations
ILC	International Law Commission
IMO	International Maritime Organisation
IPCC	Intergovernmental Panel on Climate Change
ITLOS	International Tribunal for the Law of the Sea
MARPOL	International Convention for the Prevention of Pollution from Ships
MIT	Massachusetts Institute of Technology
MPEPIL	Max Planck Encyclopaedia of Public International Law
NDC	National Determined Contribution
NGO	Non-governmental Organisation
OHCHR	Office of the United Nations High Commissioner for Human Rights
OUP	Oxford University Press
PCA	Permanent Court of Arbitration
PPP	Public-private Partnership
PUF	Presses Universitaires de France
RBDI	Revue belge de droit international
RECIEL	Review of European, Comparative & International Environmental Law

SDG	Sustainable Development Goal
SFDI	Société française pour le droit international
SPS	Sanitary and Phytosanitary
TRIPS	Trade-Related Aspects of Intellectual Property Rights
UNCLOS	United Nations Convention on the Law of the Sea
UNDDR	United Nations Office for Disaster Risk Reduction
UNDP	United Nations Development Program
UNESCO	United Nations Educational, Scientific and Cultural Organisation
UNFCCC	United Nations Framework Convention on Climate Change
UNGA	United Nations General Assembly
UNSG	United Nations Secretary General
WHA	World Health Assembly
WHO	World Health Organisation
WHO CA+	Zero draft of the WHO convention, agreement or other international instrument on pandemic prevention, preparedness and response
WTO	World Trade Organisation

Introduction

On 29 March 2023 the United Nations General Assembly, "[r]ecognising that climate change is an unprecedented challenge of civilisational proportions and that the well-being of present and future generations of humankind depends on our immediate and urgent response to it", decided to request the International Court of Justice to deliver an advisory opinion on the legal obligations of states to protect the climate system and on the legal consequences of their actions and omissions which cause harm in this regard.[1] The Commission of Small Island States on Climate Change and International Law at the end of 2022 also submitted a request for an advisory opinion to the International Tribunal for the Law of the Sea on the obligations of states parties to the United Nations Convention on the Law of the Sea to preserve the marine environment and protect it from pollution caused by adverse effects of climate change and, more generally, from impacts of this phenomenon.[2] The World Health Assembly convened a special session in December 2021, where it established an Intergovernmental Negotiating Body open to all Member States, Associate Members and regional economic integration organisations to draft and negotiate a WHO convention, agreement or other international instrument on pandemic prevention, preparedness and response.[3] In the preamble to the zero draft of this text, the parties recognise "that the international spread of disease is a global threat with serious consequences for public health, human lives, livelihoods, societies and economies that calls for the widest possible international cooperation and participation of all countries and relevant stakeholders in an effective, coordinated, appropriate and comprehensive international response".[4] These recent initiatives share some common features: they aim to address two risks that ultimately threaten the conditions of survival of humankind

1 UNGA, Request for an advisory opinion of the International Court of Justice on the obligations of States in respect of climate change, 29 March 2023, A/RES/77/276.

2 <https://www.itlos.org/fileadmin/itlos/documents/press_releases_english/PR_327_EN.pdf>. An advisory opinion has also been requested from the Interamerican Court of Human Rights on the scope of states' obligations in the prevention and limitation of the impact of climate change, Interamerican Court of Human Rights, Request for an Advisory Opinion submitted by Colombia and Chile before the Inter-American Court of Human Rights of January 9, 2023, <https://www.corteidh.or.cr/docs/opiniones/soc_1_2023_en.pdf>.

3 WHA, WHASS2/2021/REC/1, 1 December 2021.

4 Zero draft of the WHO CA+ for the consideration of the Intergovernmental Negotiating Body at its fourth meeting, WHO convention, agreement or other international instrument on pandemic prevention, preparedness and response ("WHO CA+"), 1 February 2023, A/INB/4/3, § 7.

 | DOI:10.1163/9789004538702_002

on Earth; they try to include all the different actors involved by this situation and to foster cooperation; they insist on emergency of coordinated action. International law is thus logically used to combat what amounts to global risks, and this is remarkable in a period not favourable to multilateral initiatives. But at the same time it should be kept in mind that international instruments have already been addressing the issues of climate change and epidemics for several decades without much result. In the period between the conclusion of the first legal instruments devoted to them and these current initiatives, international law has proven rather ineffective in the face of the specific features of global risks, and states have been tempted to adopt individualistic stances when faced with these challenges. But changes are underway in the way international law relates to and interacts with other legal regimes in this context, thus developing new functions. The aim of this book is precisely to analyse how the emergence of global risks affected the functioning of international law, where we are at present and what paths could be taken in the near future.

The study will focus on two global risks: climate change and pandemics. These notions need to be further clarified. More precisely, the former risk concerns the adverse effects of climate change which are defined by article 1, § 1 of the United Nations Framework Convention on Climate Change (UNFCCC) as "changes in the physical environment or biota resulting from climate change which have significant deleterious effects on the composition, resilience or productivity of natural and managed ecosystems or on the operation of socio-economic systems or on human health and welfare".[5] Since the fifth assessment report of the Intergovernmental Panel on Climate Change (IPCC), it has been well established that global warming has detrimental effects on many elements of the biosphere, including making changes in ecosystems, the acidification of oceans, rising sea levels, the number and severity of extreme climate events (storms, draughts …).[6] If some tipping points are reached in the global climate system – such as the thawing of permafrost in Antarctica – it is now established that this could lead to the inhabitability of part of the Earth and to devastating changes in the climate balance.[7]

Regarding health risks, the only existing legal notion at present is "public health emergency of international concern" which is at the core of the system

5 § 2 defines climate change as "a change of climate which is attributed directly or indirectly to human activity that alters the composition of the global atmosphere and which is in addition to natural climate variability observed over comparable time periods".

6 Intergovernmental Panel on Climate Change, "Climate Change 2014: Synthesis Report. Contribution of Working Groups I, II, and III to the Fifth Assessment Report of the Intergovernmental Panel on Climate Change".

7 IPCC, "2019 Special Report on the Ocean and Cryosphere in a Changing Climate".

of the International Health Regulations (IHR). Besides legal vocabulary, public health experts define an epidemic as an increase in the number of cases of a disease above the threshold of an endemic – meaning usual – disease.[8] The term "pandemic" refers to the global spread of the disease and it is precisely this global reach which justifies its choice in this book.

As will be discussed in the following sections, climate change and pandemics share common features with risks belonging to other fields such as economics (financial risks), security (terrorism), technology (cyber-attacks) etc. All these threats are usually referred to as "systemic" or "global" risks,[9] but they have not yet been the subject of a systematic study in international law. Existing publications – at least in English, French and Italian – deal only with one specific global risk at a time and have not yet tried to grasp the cross-sectional dimension of such risks. Some books or yearbooks address related subjects such as disaster law (which proposes a specific perspective on global risks) or the links between health and environment.[10] Other books are related to a specific global risk and eventually to its impact on international law or to another specific aspect of the phenomenon.[11] A legal definition of these risks is clearly lacking, while their effects in and on international law already exist. Moreover, the effects of global risks on the very structures of international law are also underexplored.

Even if by definition different kinds of actors, including private actors, are concerned by global risks, this book mainly focuses on public actors such as states and, to a lesser extent, on international organisations. This choice is justified by the fact that, currently, international law still primarily deals with

---

8 S. Zhou, "Some reflections on the scope of the topic "Epidemics and international law"", at 3–18 in S. Murase, S. Zhou (eds), *Epidemics and international law*, Leiden, Brill Nijhoff, 2021, XXXII–708 p.

9 See *infra*, Introduction, 2.

10 See for instance S. Negri (ed.), *Environmental health in international and EU law. Current challenges and legal responses*, Torino, G. Giappichelli Editore, 2020, XX–378 p. and G. Bartolini, D. Cubie, M. Hesselman, J. Peel (eds), *Yearbook of international disaster law*, 2018, Leiden, Brill Nijhoff.

11 See for instance on climate change: R. Rayfuse, S. V. Scott (eds), *International law in the era of climate change*, Cheltenham, Edward Elgar, 2012, XXIV–378 p.; K.R. Gray, R. Tarasofsky, C. Carlarne (eds), *The Oxford handbook of international climate change law*, OUP, 2016, XXIV–822 p.; I. Alogna, C. Bakker, J.-P. Gauci, *Climate change litigation: global perspectives*, Leiden, Brill Nijhoff, 2021, XXIV–544 p. See for instance on health risks: P. Acconci, *Tutela della salute e diritto internazionale*, Padova, CEDAM, 2011, XX–454 p.; L.O. Gostin, *Global health law*, Cambridge, Harvard University Press, 2014, XVI–542 p.; G.L. Burci, B. Toebes (eds), *Research handbook on global health law*, Cheltenham, Edward Elgar Publishing, 2018, XIV–562 p.

these public actors and, more specifically, with the fact that they have control and influence over private actors and are in a special position to coordinate the response to global risks.

This subject is introduced through some opening remarks on the practice that leads to the need to address global risks in international law (1), thus revealing the main purpose which concerns the discussion of the evolution of the functions of this legal system (2) and finally through the outline of the book's structure (3).

1 Origins of the Study

Three main reasons justify the present study. First, a legal definition of global risks is still lacking, whereas the notion is already much discussed in social sciences by sociologists and political scientists.[12] Moreover, global risks are periodically identified and debated within the United Nations[13] and in other international fora but without being based on any legal definition. The World Economic Forum delivers annually a "Global risks report" identifying the major current global risks the World is facing.[14] The most frequently mentioned risks in these contexts are financial crises, climate change, cyber-risks, terrorism and epidemics. While these agencies call for multi-stakeholders' governance built across the different sectors of knowledge, they neither mention a legal definition of these risks nor develop a specific legal analysis, whereas several international legal regimes specifically address these risks, at least in part. On the other hand, the United Nations considers that law is one of the elements to be taken into account in order to understand how structures work in risk decision systems.[15] Sustainable Development Goals (SDGs) cannot be achieved without addressing systemic risks.

Second, international law seems at first sight to be the natural means to address global risks but, quite paradoxically, states tend to try to manage them individually. Some authors for example have identified a "pandemic paradox" in relation to COVID-19: facing a crisis of global reach, states reacted by closing their borders and by taking protectionist measures, thus impairing their

---

12 See *infra*, Introduction, 2.2.

13 See for instance the Global Assessment Report for Disaster Risk Reduction of 2022: <https://www.undrr.org/gar2022-our-world-risk#container-downloads>; the Global Risk Platform of the UNPD: <https://www.undp.org/geneva/global-risk-platform>.

14 See for instance the 2022 report: <https://www3.weforum.org/docs/WEF_The_Global_Risks_Report_2022.pdf>.

15 UNDRR, Global Assessment Report for Disaster Risk Reduction of 2022, *op. cit.*, at 104.

capacity to cooperate, to control the spread of the virus and to apply equitable criteria for the distribution of vaccines and medical treatments.[16] While these risks have global reach, reactions are fragmented into multiple legal regimes at national, regional and international levels.[17] The United Nations refers to climate emergencies and pandemics such as COVID-19 as revealing a new reality which needs to be understood and tackled by all means, including legal ones.[18] The general paradox can be expressed as follows: current rapid and strong evolutions pertaining to the fact that human action has more and more global effects have broad repercussions on classical international law, which does not seem to be able to meet these challenges. One of the main difficulties lies in the fact that common concerns threatened by these risks relate to resources (the climate, public health …) situated as well within as outside states' jurisdiction. Territoriality, upon which international law is still largely grounded, thus becomes almost irrelevant. States are thus led to consider individual and non-coordinated action while being totally unable to respond to global risks on their own, for precisely the same reasons. The situation requires more international law, but probably a somewhat different one.[19]

Third, global risks pose great challenges to the very structures and main features of international law[20] by creating a situation of "organised irresponsibility" which refers to the impossibility of attributing responsibility to someone in this kind of context.[21] Global actors are so interconnected – by their actions, reactions, interactions – that every action seems to be at the same time a cause and a consequence of risks, thus rendering no one responsible for them. It then becomes impossible to assign precise responsibilities for these risks according

16 P. G. Danchin, J. Farrall, S. Rana, I. Saunders, "The pandemic paradox in international law", *AJIL*, 2020/4, at 598–607.

17 M. Delmas-Marty, *Le relatif et l'universel : les forces imaginantes du droit*, Paris, Editions du Seuil, 2004, at 353–394.

18 UNDRR, Global Assessment Report for Disaster Risk Reduction of 2022, *op. cit.*, at XIII.

19 On this paradox, see E. Brown Weiss, "Establishing norms in a kaleidoscopic world", *Collected Courses of the Hague Academy of International Law*, vol. 396, 2019, at 408.

20 The same is true for other legal systems such as domestic or regional ones, but this book specifically focuses on international law and its interactions with these other regimes.

21 U. Beck, *Risk society. Towards a new modernity*, London, SAGE Publications, 1992, at 31–32. See also A. Giddens, "Risk and Responsibility", *The Modern Law Review*, 1999, no 1, at 1–10. "Public goods entail collective action problems such as incentives for free-riding and for sub-optimal production of public goods (like prevention of global warming). "Public bads" involve overproduction of "negative externalities" (e.g. pollution) that are not "internalised" (e.g. not reflected in prices)", E.U. Petersmann, *Multilevel constitutionalism for multilevel governance of public goods: methodology problems in international law*, Oxford, Hart Publishing, 2017, at 14.

to identified legal rules, in part because often the activities causing them are not even prohibited. Taking as examples climate change and pandemics, no one seems to be immediately blameworthy for their negative consequences, but there is a conjunction of factors external to the victims that constitutes the cause of this damage. Global risks' disruptive effects on international law concern particularly interactions between global and local impacts of risk, the participation of multiple stakeholders, articulation between international law and other types of legal regimes (domestic, regional …) and the difficulties of attributing responsibility for damage produced by the occurrence of global risks.[22] Most of these legal challenges are common to other – if not all – legal orders.

2 Purpose of the Book

The main purpose is to analyse current evolutions of international law in the context of global risks through an approach of law in progress. Several authors prefer to replace the notion of "risk" with other concepts in order to address global risks. This notion can indeed be seen as linked to the rational choice philosophy and to a political agenda which emerged during the 1980s and which was based on the short-term analysis of several social phenomena.[23] Ulrich Beck points, for instance, the shortcomings of "risk-approaches" in economics, because they are based on cost-benefit analysis and tend to suggest that rational thinking could totally grasp these phenomena.[24] Moreover, this approach maintains doubt about the existence of these different kinds of threats. Several papers and institutions thus suggest using other concepts such as "disaster" or "threat". By referring to threats, many authors[25] want to make it clear that risk management tools can contribute to the dangers we face and that, on the contrary, the notion of threat insists on a reality that is

22 See on climate change, E. Fisher, E. Scotford, E. Barritt, "The Legally Disruptive Nature of Climate Change", *The Modern Law Review*, 2017, no 2, at 173–201.

23 S. Boudia, "La genèse d'un gouvernement par le risque", at 57 in D. Bourg, P.-B. Joly, A. Kaufmann (eds), *Du risque à la menace: penser la catastrophe*, Paris, PUF, 2013, X–374 p.

24 U. Beck, *op. cit.*, at 57–58 and B.M. Hutter, *Risk, resilience, inequality and environmental law*, Cheltenham, UK; Northampton, MA, USA: Edward Elgar Publishing, 2017, at 67–83.

25 D. Bourg, P.-B. Joly, A. Kaufmann, "Vingt-cinq ans après La société du risque", at 1 in D. Bourg, P.-B. Joly, A. Kaufmann (eds), *Du risque à la menace: penser la catastrophe*, Paris, PUF, 2013, X–374 p.

mostly independent of humans, which would be the case for global risks.[26] This approach seems to be too restrictive because the concept of "risk" may be considered a generic notion which is not to be systematically identified with rather recent economic approaches.

Other researchers point to the notion of disaster as developed by the International Law Commission (ILC) in its 2016 *Articles on the protection of persons in the event of disasters*. According to article 3, "'disaster' means a calamitous event or series of events resulting in widespread loss of life, great human suffering and distress, mass displacement or large-scale material or environmental damage, thereby seriously disrupting the functioning of society". This text thus encompasses the management of current disasters and, in less detail, their prevention. Moreover, its focus is on the protection of human rights with regard to disasters. In comparison with disaster, the notion of risk is centred on an anticipatory dimension and covers all possible effects of its realisation, beyond human rights issues. On the other hand, disasters share a common rationale with global risks by taking into account multiple causes and uncertainty.[27] "Climate change is the ultimate disaster".[28] The Sendai Framework for Disaster Risk Reduction (2015–2030) takes into account climate change and epidemics/pandemics as well as disaster risk drivers[29] and disasters themselves.[30] For this reason, it advocates coordination between legal tools regulating them.[31] The United Nations defines a disaster as a "serious disruption of the functioning of a community or a society at any scale due to hazardous events interacting with conditions of exposure, vulnerability and capacity, leading to one or more of the following: human, material, economic and environmental losses and impacts".[32] In this sense, this notion takes into account a combination of hazards and vulnerability criteria. Disasters indeed stem from the concurrence of several hazards with vulnerability and the exposure of people and assets;

26 A. Papaux, "De la société du risque à la société de la menace", at 145 in D. Bourg, P.-B. Joly, A. Kaufmann (eds), *Du risque à la menace: penser la catastrophe*, Paris, PUF, 2013, X–374 p.

27 R. Urueña, M.A. Prada-Uribe, "Disasters, inter-State legal obligations, and the risk society: the contribution of the ILC's draft articles", at 70 in G. Bartolini, D. Cubie, M. Hesselman, J. Peel (eds), *Yearbook of international disaster law*, 2018, Brill Nijhoff, 2020, VIII–516 p.

28 J. McDonald, A. Telesetsky, "Disaster by degrees: the implications of the IPCC 1,5°C report for disaster law", at 179 in G. Bartolini, D. Cubie, M. Hesselman, J. Peel (eds), *Yearbook of international disaster law*, 2018, Brill Nijhoff, 2020, VIII–516 p.

29 § 4.

30 § 28.

31 See also CCNUCC, Report on the expert meeting on national adaptation goals/indicators and their relationship with the SDG and the Sendai framework for disaster risk reduction, AC/2018/13, 16 October 2018.

32 UNDRR, Global Assessment Report for Disaster Risk Reduction of 2022, *op. cit.*, at 2.

they point to the *result* of the occurrence of risks. In summary, the concept of threat does not focus on anthropogenic causes and the concept of disaster refers to the result of the occurrence of a risk, thus taking little account of the need for anticipation. The notion of risk seems more suitable than these two alternative concepts to the approach chosen; it will thus be used in this work.

In order to analyse the current challenges international law is facing because of global risks, the perspective chosen is the relationship between international law and domestic legal regimes. The global dimension of these risks entails interactions between different stakeholders and different levels of action: international, regional, domestic, transnational ... In this context, first, all these legal regimes face similar challenges – notably on responsibility issues – and, second, their relationships tend to develop as their interplay is necessary for one fully to grasp global risks. For this reason, the argument is based on international law, but also on several domestic law sources and, above all, on litigation and case law. This book thus adopts Edith Brown Weiss's remark about "the transition we are now undergoing to a new international system"[33] and takes it as a starting point.

As already mentioned, the present study is based on the practice related more specifically to two global risks: climate change and pandemics. Even if all systemic risks tend to be related, climate change and pandemics have complex and close links that justify their joint study.[34] Climate change is such a diffuse phenomenon that it has consequences in all areas and finally threatens our own existence.[35] Domestic litigation against states on climate change and pandemic risks is largely discussed in the book and, even if there is no pretence of completeness, the case law of all continents is taken into account. All the case studied may be found – most often with an English translation – on two online databases.[36] Even if climate and health litigation may have several kinds of objects, here the cases chosen share some common features: they all focus on states' insufficient action in the prevention or reaction to global risks

33 E. Brown Weiss, *op. cit.*, at 408.

34 See *infra*, Introduction, 4.

35 R. Rayfuse, S. V. Scott, "Mapping the impact of climate change on international law", at 6 in R. Rayfuse, S. V. Scott (eds), *International law in the era of climate change*, Cheltenham; Northampton Mass: Edward Elgar, 2012, XXIV–378 p.

36 Two databases are used in order to access domestic case law: climate litigation – when necessary, translated into English – may be found on the Sabin Centre of Columbia University database: <http://climatecasechart.com/>. Litigation related to the COVID-19 pandemic is updated and presented in the framework of a research project carried out by a partnership including several national and international institutions: <https://www.COVID19litigation.org/about>.

aimed at limiting the damage produced by some of their effects; the object of legal actions may be either the declaration of the responsibility of a state or judicial review of state legal acts; all claims are at least partly based on the implementation of international law commitments in the fight against global risks.

Finally, the book discusses only the risk dimension which entails anticipation, before the (complete) occurrence of damage. It does not analyse the rules pertaining to the management of the effects produced by the realisation of global risks.[37] The risk addressed in relation to climate change is its adverse effects, among which are the multiplication of extreme weather events (floods, droughts, temperature peaks, cyclones), slower transformations such as the disappearance of certain territories, the modification of ecosystems caused by sea level rise, the scarcity of many vital resources such as drinking water, the multiplication of health problems for humans ... For the sake of clarity, the risk related to these adverse effects is referred to as the "climate change risk". The emergence and spread of pandemics due to new pathogens such as COVID-19 also potentially entails a series of adverse effects on all human activities.

The main argument is that several functions and structures of international law are evolving because of the need to address global risks which have consequences worldwide and in all areas of life. Legally speaking, interactions between domestic, regional and international rules and institutions are creating transnational "spaces" devoted to the regulation of these risks involving the various stakeholders, even if the situations vary greatly depending on each type of risk. The examples of climate change and pandemics are studied as illustrations of this phenomenon which, according to Edith Brown Weiss, characterises a "kaleidoscopic world".[38]

3 Structure of the Book

The first chapter develops the elements of a legal definition of global risks. While the notions of risk and of hazardous activities are not new, several characteristics of what we recognise as global risks have emerged with the globalisation process and create specific challenges. The notion of systemic risks as developed and studied in other fields – both of hard and social sciences – is a useful starting point for defining a legal approach to this phenomenon. A specific development is devoted to the peculiar and multi-faceted relations

37 Which is more in line with the disaster law approach.

38 E. Brown Weiss, *op. cit.*

existing between the two global risks that are the objects of this book: climate change and pandemics. This is an example of intersection between systemic risks which is starting to be taken into account through the One Health approach.

The second chapter deals with the function of international law in relation to these global risks and to the various ways in which it addresses them. Legal norms and institutions related to global risks seem to be rather fragmented, thus making it more difficult for international law to respond to their key challenges. Some legal tools are used in order to address the peculiarities of global risks, and this is the case, for example, of due diligence as a catalyst of international obligations and as a bridge between legal regimes. Other tools are introduced with the specific aim of tackling challenges posed by global risks; the example of the integration principle is here extensively studied.

The third chapter focuses on responsibilities for global risks, drawing on a wide approach. While the rules of the international responsibility of states and international organisations do not seem appropriate to the characteristics of global risks, some hints have been provided by responsibility regimes for the violation of human rights in this context. Most important, domestic courts all around the world are developing what seems to be a new legal regime of responsibility for global risks which could be a source of inspiration also at the international level.

The fourth and last chapter adopts a prospective perspective in order to imagine what could be the consequences of the development of the emerging solidarity principle in relation to global risks. Climate and public health are beginning to be taken into account as global public goods, this notion having some legal effects on the definition of their protection; it also follows from this approach that new rationales are introduced into several international legal regimes, the focus of which is on the principle of mutual supportiveness.

Each chapter concludes with a short discussion on whether the findings seem *prima facie* to be relevant also to other global risks and a general conclusion draws on the main paths of evolution of the function of international law in relation to global risks.

CHAPTER 1

International Legal Concept of Global Risk

1 Introduction

Systemic risks have been studied for several years in both hard and social sciences, but this phenomenon has surprisingly been rather ignored in the legal field, where it also has a great impact. While these risks point to phenomena already known in recent centuries, they have developed new dimensions due mainly to the more recent globalisation process. Human action is thus creating more risks, and above all more dangerous risks, because for the first time in history they have a bearing on the potential destruction of humankind and a major change in the physical characteristics of the Earth – or at least in living conditions on Earth (2). Starting from the works in several other research fields, it is possible to identify legal elements of the definition of global risks which allow one both to understand better their disruptive potential in international law and to have a basis for addressing this phenomenon in legal thinking (3). Among these risks, climate change and pandemics are studied together for a series of reasons including their peculiar and multi-faceted relationship, which has in part been revealed by the COVID-19 pandemic (4).

2 The Background: What Is New?

The notion of risk can be generally defined as the probability of the occurrence of an adverse event with negative impacts.[1] The concepts of risk and hazardous or even ultra-hazardous activities have been well known to legal scholars and in legal practice at least since the industrial revolution. They have led to the creation of insurance mechanisms currently used worldwide. The types of risks addressed in this book have also been known for centuries. During the 18th and the 19th centuries, for example, many studies focused on climate variations and on the role of humans in this phenomenon, mainly related to

1 The Oxford Learner's Dictionaries defines risk as "the possibility of something bad happening at some time in the future; a situation that could be dangerous or have a bad result", <https://www.oxfordlearnersdictionaries.com/definition/english/risk_1#:~:text=%2Fr%C9%AAsk%2F-,%2Fr%C9%AAsk%2F,or%20have%20a%20bad%20result>.

 | DOI:10.1163/9789004538702_003

deforestation.[2] Risks of epidemics and pandemics have also been known and studied at least since the 19th century and the causes of infectious diseases have often been the subject of scientific controversy in the past.[3] Indeed, epidemics have never been reduced to biological causes and have always involved environmental, social and political factors. Several causes have, however, provoked a drastic change not in the nature but in the dimensions of risks that were identified as a new category at the end of the 20th century in different fields (2.1), before becoming a central issue in social sciences (2.2).

2.1 *The Origins of Studies on Global Risks*

Global risks – which are one of the consequences of the current process of globalisation – emerged rather late, at the end of the 20th century, in the context of what is referred to as the "Anthropocene". The Anthropocene Epoch is an expression used to describe the most recent period in Earth's history when human activity started to have a significant impact on the planet's climate and on ecosystems. The term was coined by a few researchers including the chemist Paul Crutzen in the early 2000s.[4] The unique and defining feature of this epoch is that humans are refashioning natural processes mainly by accelerating them.[5] In this context, the main features of global risks are that they entail a high level of uncertainty and that they are likely to have existential effects by threatening our own existence; climate risks, for instance, were already being addressed during the 19th century, but we are actually facing a new dimension. They are also irreversible and long-term in nature. The main features of current risks follow from a disruption of space-time boundaries: they are shifting and impossible to predict. Ulrich Beck characterises global risks by delocalisation, incalculability and non-compensatability.[6] Boundaries and relationships are transformed through transnational processes. From a spatial point of view, it is thus necessary to go beyond the reasoning based on the source of the risk. Jean-Pierre Galland, for instance, classifies risks as "territorialised", "diffuse", "networked", each category having a different link with

2 J.-B. Fressoz, D. Pestré, "Risque et société du risque depuis deux siècles", at 22 in D. Bourg, P.-B. Joly, A. Kaufmann (eds), *Du risque à la menace: penser la catastrophe*, Paris, PUF, 2013, x–374 p.

3 F. Vagneron, P. Bourdelais, "Understandings of disease transmission in the Western World", in B. Delaurenti, T. Le Roux (eds), *Cultures of contagion*, MIT Press, Cambridge, London, 2021, at 165–170.

4 P. Crutzen, E. Stoermer, "The "Anthropocene"", *International Geosphere-Biosphere Programme Newsletter*, vol. 14 (May 2000), at 17, <http://www.igbp.net>.

5 E. Brown Weiss, *op. cit.*, at 64.

6 U. Beck, *op. cit.*, at 36–37.

the state's territory.[7] Earth's climate system is extremely complex because it depends on multiple elements such as laws of conservation, but also on the interdependence between interrelated physical and chemical processes that need to be modelled by scientists. The global spread of new pathogens resulting in a pandemic is also unpredictable because it depends on a series of interconnected factors at different spatial levels.[8] This new dimension was, for example, taken into account during the revision of the International Health Regulations (IHR) in 2005 by the introduction of new implementation criteria based on the transnational dimension of pandemics.

This current evolution is greatly influenced by the process of globalisation[9] leading to the emergence of several transnational risks depending on the growing interdependence and development of exchanges favouring the spread of infectious diseases, the increase in the toxicity of the environment, the multiplication of different types of accidents in connection with technological advances[10] …

The identification of "global systemic risks" reflects the fact that modern societies have a high level of interconnections between different sectors, which poses intrinsic so-called systemic risks due to "feedbacks between all parts of the global socio-environmental system".[11] These risks were first modelled by hard science and social science works. From the point of view of physicians, for instance, "systemic risk is the risk of having not just statistically independent failures, but interdependent, so-called 'cascading' failures in a network of *N* interconnected system components. That is, systemic risks result from con-

---

7 Quoted by V. November, "La spatialité des risques dans une société du risque et après", at 280 in D. Bourg, P.-B. Joly, A. Kaufmann (eds), *Du risque à la menace: penser la catastrophe*, Paris, PUF, 2013, X–374 p.

8 J. Kay, M. King, "The Radical Uncertainties of Coronavirus", *Prospect Magazine*, 2020 <www.prospectmagazine.co.uk/magazine/coronavirus-model-uncertainty-kay-king>.

9 "Globalisation can generally be understood as the process driven by and resulting in increased cross-border flows of goods, services, money, people, information, technology, and culture", I. Goldin, M. Mariathasan, *The Butterfly Defect. How globalisation creates systemic risks, and what to do about it*, Princeton University Press, 2014, at 10.

10 F. Vagneron, "Les épidémies ne se réduisent jamais à des causes biologiques", *Le Monde*, 25 January 2022, <https://journal.lemonde.fr/data/1872/reader/reader.html?t=1643115050164#!preferred/0/package/1872/pub/2546/page/14/alb/118825>. He points to the role of the unprecedented globalisation of trade and movement in the spread of epidemics such as COVID-19.

11 "[…] rétroactions entre toutes les parties du système socio-environnemental global", P.-Y. Longaretti, "Risques systémiques globaux et risques d'effondrement. Quels éléments d'analyse scientifique, pour quels types de risques?", *LIREC Lettre d'Information sur les Risques et Crises*, Institut national des hautes études de la sécurité et de la justice (INHESJ), 2020, at 5. My translation.

nections between risks ('networked risks'). In such cases, a localised initial failure ('perturbation') could have disastrous effects and cause, in principle, unbounded damage as N goes to infinity".[12] Systemic risks are created by networks which favour the rapid global spread of dangerous events that can lead to disasters. Dirk Helbing points to risks related to the environment, to health, to financial systems, to supply chains and to information and communication systems. For example, the spread of an epidemic is the result, among other factors, of interconnections and air traffic, and it has serious effects on health, economics and social life. In order to grasp these new risks, experts consider it necessary to adopt a new perspective centred on interactions between systems and networks.[13] Most researchers agree on the identification of five categories of global risks: economic (due to market instability and to finance), geopolitical (due to sources of instability and above all terrorism), environmental (due to climate change, natural disasters, loss of biodiversity), societal (due to health threats, migration flows and inequalities) and technological (due to the fragility of computerised communication systems and networked infrastructures).[14]

2.2 *Global Risks in Social Sciences*

Turning to social sciences, following the leading works of Ulrich Beck and Anthony Giddens, sociologists continue to study global risks and the risk society.[15] They define "the global system as a set of tightly coupled interactions that allow for the continued flow of information, money, good"[16] and systemic risk as a "threat that individual failures, accidents, or disruptions present to a system through the process of contagion".[17] Threats thus become networked and have to be analysed using a new lens.[18] Anthony Giddens refers to "manufactured

12 D. Helbing, "Globally Networked Risks and how to Respond", *Nature*, 2013, at 51.

13 "Global Systems Science wants to make the theory of complex systems applicable to the solution of global-scale problems. It will take a massively data-driven approach that builds on a serious collaboration between the natural, engineering, and social sciences, aiming at a grand integration of knowledge", D. Helbing, *op. cit.*, at 51.

14 P.-Y. Longaretti, *op. cit.*, at 5.

15 "A risk society is a society where we increasingly live on a high technological frontier which absolutely no one completely understands and which generates a diversity of possible futures", A. Giddens, *op. cit.*, at 3.

16 M.A. Centeno, M. Nag, T.S. Patterson, A. Shaver, A.J. Windawi, "The emergence of global systemic risk", *Annual Review of Sociology*, 2015, at 66.

17 *Ibid.*, at 68.

18 See E. Morin, "Au-delà du réductionnisme et du holisme: la complexité du global", at 441–447 in M. Wieviorka, L. Lévi-Strauss, G. Lieppe (eds), *Penser global. Internationalisation et globalisation des sciences humaines et sociales*, Maison des Sciences de l'Homme, 2015, 480 p.

risk" which is created by the progression of human development and which, for the first time in history, has the capacity to destroy our own existence.[19] Sociologists also point to the challenges of global risks for responsibility because the links between risk, decision – meaning power – and responsibility are totally altered.[20] As noted above, Ulrich Beck in this context develops the idea of organised irresponsibility, meaning that risks are produced by the actions and omissions of several actors but without the possibility of their being held accountable for them because, in their different spheres of action, they are considered lawful and even desirable or beneficial.[21]

Economic experts have also extensively addressed "integrated global relationships and systems" which include infrastructure, finance, transport, information, economics and business.[22] While they agree that the nature of the risks is not new, they also point to the two characteristics of interdependence and of existential effects. They insist on the spillover effects of individual activities and on the unpredictability of the effects of systemic risks. Complexity describes "phenomena generated by interacting parts, all of whose causal connections are not easily discernible, [and] whose behaviour over time exhibits disorder and behaves unpredictably or chaotically".[23] Our current interdependence is so high that it has been calculated according to the main models that a global pandemic could be avoided only with the vaccination of 75 per cent of the world's population if taking two plane journeys on average into account; the current traffic would require global vaccination.[24] This is the first time that we reach a degree of interdependence drastically reducing our capacity to make well-informed decisions. Current international institutions are not prepared for unpredictable circumstances. One of the conclusions of economists is that these different risks must be tackled together and that fragmented regulation of environmental risks is ineffective.

The second element consists in the existential consequences of the occurrence of systemic risks. "Systemic risk refers to the prospect of a *breakdown in the entire system* as opposed to the breakdown of individual parts".[25]

19 A. Giddens, *op. cit.*, at 4.

20 *Ibid.*, at 8.

21 U. Beck, *op. cit.*, at 58–59.

22 I. Goldin, M. Mariathasan, *op. cit.*, at 2.

23 *Ibid.*, at 19.

24 "The complexity of global travel and global integration mean that any 'patient zero' is now but a few degrees of separation from formerly isolated communities", *ibid.*, at 145.

25 *Ibid.*, at 27.

Environmental risks are thus peculiar because they entail potential "devastating second-round effects"[26] extending well beyond the original risk.

Facing these risks, the main proposals of economists are to define the following guiding principles of management: transparency, inclusivity and resilience in policies at the local, national and global levels, following the principle of subsidiarity. Six lessons are drawn from this by Ian Goldin and Mike Mariathasan: first, to take into consideration "the broader context and longer time horizons".[27] This way, the greater costs in the short term are offset by the benefits of being able to respond to unforeseen risks. Second, to acknowledge uncertainties publicly in order to communicate on them and to create processes suited to take complexity into account. Third, not to be over-reliant on models and calculations because of the incompressible margin of uncertainty. Fourth, to develop more inclusive economic analysis taking into account external interests, even on the part of private actors. Fifth, to develop plans to prepare for contingencies and to integrate this necessity in all decision-making processes. Sixth, to create unified legal responsibilities involving all stakeholders for the global and local management of systemic risks.

In short, a consensus across different research fields can be found on the fact that the novelty lies in two characteristics of global risks. First, they are not new risks by nature, but globalisation multiplies them, creates interactions between them and dramatically increases the margin of uncertainty to be taken into account in order to face them.[28] Our institutions and rules at the domestic, regional and international levels are not prepared to face this challenge and to tackle the current situation. Second, global risks' long-term effects are particularly serious both qualitatively – the damage they produce is irreversible and threatens our own existence – and quantitatively – their interwoven effects have worldwide reach. Climate change and pandemics thus have polycentric causes and consequences depending on the cumulative and indirect effects of human activities across a range of sectors, at different scales, in different countries.[29]

---

26 *Ibid.*, at 130.

27 For hospitals in order to face pandemics it would mean creating "higher reserves of medical supplies and treatment capacity", *ibid.*, at 212–214.

28 M. Delmas-Marty, *Le relatif et l'universel: les forces imaginantes du droit*, *op. cit.*, at 356.

29 See, among others, E. Fisher, E. Scotford, E. Barritt, *op. cit.*, at 178.

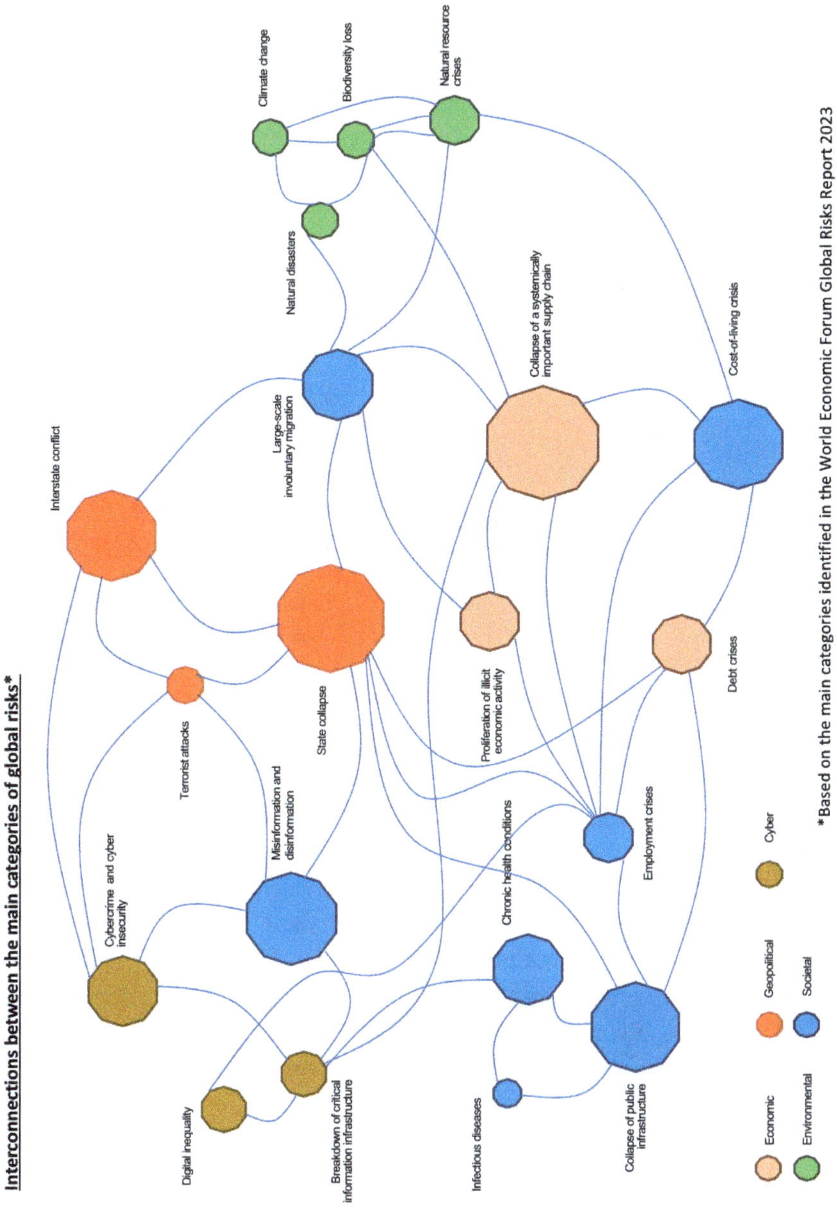

FIGURE 1 Interconnections between global risks

3 Elements of a Legal Definition of Global Risks

Starting from Ulrich Beck's work on global risks in sociology, this section deals with the criteria of a legal definition. Beck considers that our time, since the end of the 20th century, is defined as an "industrial society of risk" which is characterised by an immanent trend to globalise risks.[30] Threats become universal regardless of their origin. In the past, lawyers have already faced the challenge of the emergence of new kinds of risks, for example after the industrial revolution. At that time, the seriousness of the consequences of these risks and the fact that they were caused by lawful activities which were even beneficial to and promoted by the whole of society led to the creation of collective legal tools such as insurance mechanisms and regimes of strict liability. Ulrich Beck has shown that, while the industrial society was built at the end of the 19th century in opposition to the traditional agrarian society, the risk society is inherently self-destructive and thus built against its own model.[31] In this perspective, global risks constitute a new turning point, bringing to light the shortfalls of our current legal instruments in all legal systems, whether international, domestic or regional.

The global character of risks – which challenges the implementation of law in their regard – is present at two levels also through a legal perspective: their origins and their effects. In this field too, global risks are then identified by the interconnection between (and thus by the indeterminacy of) their causes (3.1) and by the seriousness of their effects (3.2).

3.1 *Defining Features Related to the Origins of Global Risks*

Regarding their origins, global risks are defined by three characteristics: they have multiple and heterogeneous causes pertaining mainly to lawful activities, these causes include the actions and omissions of a plurality and diversity of actors and every single action or omission is likely to have global resonance.[32] These elements characterise the risks of both climate change and pandemics. Starting with climate change, first, variations in temperature and weather conditions over the long term are the result of several kinds of factors, including natural processes, but since the beginning of the 19th century they have been mainly the result of human activity, especially the use of fossil fuels – such as

30 U. Beck, *op. cit.*, at 36.

31 *Ibid.*, at 22.

32 "[W]hat we do in one place, either individually or cumulatively, can significantly affect both the local and the global resilience and integrity of our planet": E. Brown Weiss, *op. cit.*, at 64–65.

coal, oil and gas – which produce GHGs. Most human activities at the origin of GHG emissions are not only lawful but even considered to be largely beneficial, as is the case in the sectors of the production of energy, transport, agriculture, the building industry ... Second, actors responsible – more or less directly – for the anthropogenic part of this warming are also located at the global level: companies (especially transnational ones), individuals, states, international organisations, etc. More precisely, it is their interaction that contributes to this phenomenon: some of them are direct emitters of GHGs, while others have the normative or executive power to control or even to limit their production. This interaction appears, for example, in the relations between the European Union, its member states and private actors under their jurisdiction.[33] Third, climate interdependence is such that the emission of greenhouse gases from any location has cascading consequences with a global reach. The same is true of omissions in preventing GHG emissions on the part of states for example: the negligence of a specific state has effects on the situation of all other countries. For this reason, some small developing island states have announced their will to initiate international disputes against the states having jurisdiction over the larger GHG emitters.[34] Domestic courts have also extensively addressed the issue of the global reach of state inaction and, conversely, of the need for the sake of the whole of the world's population for every state to contribute to the fight against climate change.[35]

As regards pandemics, first, they are also provoked by both natural and human causes; the emergence of a new pathogen may be linked to environmental exposure, but the most recent pandemics all have zoonotic origins that may be favoured by the multiplication of spaces where humans are in contact with wild animals. Research activities may also be a cause of the emergence of pathogens in medical laboratories or of their accidental spread during transport, for example. Here, too, most of the activities which may contribute to a pandemic risk are lawful and beneficial: that is the case, for example, of medical research, of transport, of trade etc.

---

33 S. Cassella, "Responsabilité(s) de l'Etat pour le risque global lié aux changements climatiques", *Revue générale de droit international public*, 2019/2, at 356.

34 See for instance, on the initiative of Vanuatu, M. Wewerinke-Singh, D. Hinge Salili, "Between negotiations and litigation: Vanuatu's perspective on loss and damage from climate change", *Climate policy*, 2019, <https://doi.org/10.1080/14693062.2019.1623166>.

35 See for instance, and among other cases, United States Supreme Court, *Massachusetts et al. v. Environmental protection agency et al.* (*Massachusetts v. EPA*), 2 April 2007, at 4. This issue was also clearly addressed by The Hague District Court, *Urgenda Foundation v. State of the Netherlands*, 24 June 2015, § 4.79.

Second, the outbreak and spread of a pandemic also depend on the actions and omissions of various private actors (individuals, medical institutions, doctors and medical staff, transporters) of the state where the infectious agent first appears and of all the other states which react in different ways to the health emergency, of international organisations involved (mainly the WHO). Here too, some of these actors' actions are at the origin of the pandemic, but also some actors' omissions or negligence are. States, for example, have at least the power to take preventative measures on their territory and the WHO assumes a coordinating and normative function as soon as it has identified a situation which may constitute a public health emergency of international concern. Third, the actions and omissions of the actors involved potentially have a planetary reach. For example, although the origin of the COVID-19 pandemic is not yet clear, it seems that China's omissions regarding its information duties at the end of 2019, other states' reactions to the spread of the disease, the WHO's late action etc. have all contributed in part to the outbreak and to the spread of the pandemic.[36] For example, the fact that several states at the beginning of the COVID-19 pandemic refused to take restrictive measures in order to foster herd immunity probably accelerated the emergence of virus variants that soon circulated worldwide.

From a legal perspective, these three features entail a concurrence between different causes of risk, a specific causal nexus between the various actions and omissions of interdependent actors and a particularly wide reach of each of these actions and omissions. The other characteristics of global risks having legal relevance relate to their effects.

3.2 *Defining Features Related to the Potential Effects of Global Risks*

Concerning the effects of their occurrence, global risks also have three main characteristics: they affect "global public goods," or at least resources of common concern (as provided by several treaties),[37] the total damage they produce can be evaluated only by taking into account the accumulation of specific damage in different fields over space and time – including damage produced by reactions to global risks – and they affect many and varying legally protected interests. The conjunction of these features leads to the seriousness of effects they have which are likely to threaten elements necessary to the existence of humanity. As regards climate change, first the damage is necessarily collective and general, in the sense that it affects climate – a collective good – and

36 S. Cassella, "La responsabilité des Etats et des organisations internationales du fait de la pandémie de COVID-19", *Annuaire français de droit international*, 2020, at 51–70.

37 See *infra*, Chapter 4, 2.2.

thus the whole of the international community, albeit with varying degrees of intensity depending on a number of parameters, including the capacity of each state to adapt to climate change. Second, the irreversible damage is generated by the accumulation in space and time of GHG emissions leading to climate change and possibly by bad choices of measures aimed at combatting it, such as geo-engineering. Third, this damage affects many different rights and interests, including the environment, different types of human rights, human and animal health, economic interests, etc. The various reports of the IPCC extensively analyse models of the accumulation of emissions – also by taking into account the function of carbon sinks or reservoirs – and detail the various types of harm that can be linked to adverse effects of climate change.[38]

Pandemic risk can be analysed in a similar fashion: first, its realisation seriously affects, in particular, human health which can be considered a common good. Second, the final harm – a large part of which is irreversible – is the result of the accumulation in time and space of harms both directly caused by the pandemic and indirectly aggravated by measures taken in order to fight it. Many casualties could, for example, probably have been avoided if the COVID-19 vaccine had been better distributed among the different countries in 2021. Third, these harms affect several kinds of interests such as the protection of life, health, many fundamental rights and freedoms, economic rights ...

From a legal perspective, the effects of global risks involve a common interest of the international community: the complex harm they produce is the result of an accumulation of incidents of partial damage; their adverse effects cover several kinds of interests legally protected.

It is important to insist on the difference between the overall risk and the damage that can be produced by its occurrence. The defining features discussed here are linked to the types of risks and to all their global aspects, and not to each kind of damage they may – virtually – entail. For example, food safety may be threatened as much by climate change as by pandemics, but this does not mean that there is a "food safety global risk". Food safety may sometimes depend only on national – or regional – supply and on national conditions, even if that is often not the case because of interdependence between countries. Food safety may be understood as a common concern, but its preservation does not necessarily need the participation of all levels of action and of many stakeholders. On the contrary, climate change and pandemics are by definition global phenomena and the preservation of the public goods concerned (climate stability and public health) requires the participation of all

38 See in particular IPCC, "AR6 Synthesis Report - Climate Change 2023", <https://www.ipcc.ch/report/ar6/syr/>.

global actors. Unlike other types of risk, their defining elements can never be limited to a specific area or identifiable community.

These new global risks create challenges for all legal systems – domestic, regional, international – which are not designed to take all these parameters and their interactions into account: neither can grasp complex causality, multiple responsibilities, local and global damage or even the links between all the legitimate interests at stake. This is why we need to rethink several legal concepts through this cross-cutting dimension, in order to take into account the interactions and interdependence between all the criteria of global risks.[39] Whatever the perspective of analysis of global risks, they have the specificity to produce effects beyond the frame of reference of each discipline: geographical borders, economic sectors, legal systems[40] etc. Legal answers to global risks should adapt to the main characteristics which define them; lawyers should develop tools enabling them to take indeterminacy and interconnectedness into account. Legal challenges and legal evolutions created by global risks cannot be understood without a prior definition of their distinctive features. The United Nations point, moreover, to the need to develop a common "risk language" and a set of interoperable standards across systems and disciplines which deal with global risks.[41] The main purpose here is to show how they already have a disruptive effect on the function of international law in relation to other legal systems.

4 Relationship between the Risks of Climate Change and Pandemics

Besides their common characteristics defining them as global risks, climate change and pandemics have some different features regarding, in particular, the temporality of their realisation: both are characterised by a combination of short-term (acute) and long-term (diffuse) effects, but not in the same proportion.[42] Climate change is above all a long-lasting phenomenon that produces an accumulation of damage in the long term; pandemics develop in more or less short "crises" even if it is extremely difficult to identify the "end" of a

39 M. Hautereau-Boutonnet, "Quel droit climatique ?", *Rec. Dalloz*, 2015, at 2260.

40 UNDRR, Global Assessment Report on Disaster Risk Reduction, *op. cit.*, at 4.

41 *Ibid.*, at 1.

42 Some authors consider it a paradox to perceive climate change as a long-term risk and epidemics as short-term risks because this approach could precisely hinder their specific relationship. See I.A. Giménez, "Epidemics and climate change in international law", at 411–434 in S. Murase, S. Zhou (eds), *Epidemics and international law*, Leiden, Brill Nijhoff, 2021, XXXII–708 p.

pandemic or the extinction of its effects.[43] The origin of their global dimension also varies: climate change is intrinsically global because climate is a global system; in contrast, a pandemic is the result of the inevitable spread of a pathogen that first appears in a specific place. In this latter case the global dimension is mainly due to the current level of interconnectedness of human activities.

But these risks also interact in various ways;[44] all recent epidemics, for example, are linked to the interrelations between human health issues, animal health issues and the degradation of the environment.[45] Generally speaking, climate change has different links to health, but the focus here is on the relationship between the two global risks. First, when occurring these risks influence each other's evolution and this factual link is currently studied by experts in both fields who recommend addressing them together (4.1). This link is starting to be taken into account by the legal regimes devoted to these two risks, each one of them tending progressively to integrate some elements of the other risk (4.2). The first substantive consequence of the interaction between climate change and health is the emergence of the human right to a healthy and sustainable environment (4.3).

4.1 *Cross Influences*

On one side, climate change is one of the causes of the emergence of new pathogens the spread of which can lead to a pandemic, and it tends to modify their conditions of transmission. The effect of climate on epidemics has long been recognised[46] but has evolved in the context of the acceleration of GHG emissions and is currently studied using a risk analysis perspective. In his 2018 report on "Health, environment and climate change", the Director general of the WHO recognises the new environmental and health challenges by stating that environmental risks create direct health impacts of emergencies and the expansion of infectious disease risks.[47] The WHO has thus started to admit that

43 On this issue, see F. Paddeu, M. Waibel, "The Final Act: Exploring the End of Pandemics", *AJIL*, 2020/4, at 698–707.

44 The UN Special Rapporteur on human rights and the environment refers to "interlinked global crises": D.R. Boyd, "Report of the Special Rapporteur on the issue of human rights obligations relating to the enjoyment of a safe, clean, healthy and sustainable environment – The human right to a clean, healthy and sustainable environment: a catalyst for accelerated action to achieve the Sustainable Development Goals", 10 August 2022, A/77/284, § 3.

45 F. Vagneron, "Les épidémies ne se réduisent jamais à des causes biologiques", *op. cit.*

46 "Smallpox and climate", *American Journal of Public Health*, 1926, at 1027–1029.

47 WHO, Report of the Director General on "Health, environment and climate change", 9 April 2018, A71/10.

the greatest threat to human health in the 21st century is posed by climate change which in part has human causes: "[c]limate change is […] modifying the transmission of food-borne, water-borne and zoonotic infectious diseases, resulting in large impacts on health".[48] More precisely, it is now scientifically proved that the risk of pandemics consisting in zoonoses is caused by a series of human activities, including those leading to climate change.[49]

On the other hand, pandemics contribute to the degradation of the ecosystem (even if not the climate as such) in parallel with climate change; as stated by the Manhattan Principles on "One World, One Health" – issued by a symposium of health experts organised by the Wildlife Conservation Society – "[t]he rise of emerging and resurging infectious diseases threatens not only humans […], but also the fauna and flora comprising the critically needed biodiversity that supports the living infrastructure of our world".[50] The "One Health" approach tends to build on the acknowledgment of this interrelationship between global risks in order to address them in a mutually supportive way.[51] The United Nations Sendai Framework for Disaster Risk Reduction (2015–2030) also builds on this link in order to ensure coherence between the prevention and the management of climate and health disasters. The Bangkok principles for the implementation of the health aspects of the Sendai framework, in particular, aim to "strengthen the integration of biological hazards, including epidemics, pandemics, and diseases at the human-animal-ecosystem interface, into all-hazards multi-sectoral disaster risk management".[52] According to the WHO Global Strategy on Health, Environment and Climate Change, an "integrated and mainstreamed approach across all sectors" is needed in order to tackle these challenges together.[53] This means that climate risks should be taken into account above everything else in the domestic implementation of

48 WHO Global Strategy on Health, Environment and Climate Change, 2020, § 7.

49 B.A. Jones and others, "Zoonosis emergence linked to agricultural intensification and environmental change", *Proceedings of the National Academy of Science*, vol. 110, No. 21, 21 May 2013. See also D.R. Boyd, Report of the Special Rapporteur on the issue of human rights obligations relating to the enjoyment of a safe, clean, healthy and sustainable environment, 15 July 2020, A/75/161, § 11.

50 The Manhattan Principles on "One World, One Health", preamble, <https://oneworldonehealth.wcs.org/About-Us/Mission/The-Manhattan-Principles.aspx>.

51 See among others S. Negri, *Salute pubblica, sicurezza e diritti umani nel diritto internazionale*, Torino, G. Giappichelli Editore, 2018, at 176.

52 Principle 1, <https://www.preventionweb.net/files/47606_bangkokprinciplesfortheimplementati.pdf>. See also S. Negri, "International health law", at 445 in G. Bartolini, D. Cubie, M. Hesselman, J. Peel (eds), *Yearbook of international disaster law*, 2018, Brill Nijhoff, 2020, VIII–516 p.

53 *Op. cit.*, § 17.

international health instruments and that health risks should be included in the assessment accompanying the domestic implementation of climate protection measures. The UN Sustainable Development Goals have been elaborated in order to address the main current global challenges through concerted action, including by implementing human rights and environmental state obligations together.[54] Experts tend to point to climate change and epidemics as the two most pressing global threats and emphasise that neither can be totally grasped by referring only to the international legal regime devoted to its management.[55]

4.2 *Legal Means of Coordination in the Fight against the Two Risks*

Coordination means can be found, first, in the legal instruments devoted to health protection. The environment is seen as a determinant of the right to health, from which flow indirect state obligations to protect the environment and in particular to combat climate change. According to the Committee on economic, social and cultural rights, "the right to health embraces a wide range of socio-economic factors that promote conditions in which people can lead a healthy life, and extends to the underlying determinants of health, such as food and nutrition, housing, access to safe and potable water and adequate sanitation, safe and healthy working conditions, and a healthy environment".[56] As regards obligations to respect the right to health, the Committee affirms that to refrain from unlawfully polluting air, water and soil.[57] Among state obligations to fulfil the right to health, the Committee identifies the need to adopt measures preventing environmental health hazards such as the formulation and implementation of national policies aimed at reducing and eliminating pollution (including air pollution).[58] The Committee on the Rights of the Child also addresses the environment as a determinant of health and insists more specifically on the climate obligations of states: "[e]nvironmental interventions

---

54 D.R. Boyd, "Report of the Special Rapporteur on the issue of human rights obligations relating to the enjoyment of a safe, clean, healthy and sustainable environment – The human right to a clean, healthy and sustainable environment: a catalyst for accelerated action to achieve the Sustainable Development Goals", *op. cit.*, § 6.

55 I.A. Giménez, *op. cit.*

56 CESCR, General Comment No 14 (2000): The Right to the Highest Attainable Standard of Health (Article 12 of the International Covenant on Economic, Social and Cultural Rights), § 4. See also the decision of the African Commission on human and people's rights, *Sudan Human Rights Organisation & Centre on Housing Rights and Evictions* (COHRE) *v. Sudan*, 27 May 2009, which recognises developments in the right to health and in particular the environment as health determinant.

57 CESCR, General Comment No 14 (2000), *op. cit.*, § 34.

58 *Ibid.*, § 36.

should, inter alia, address climate change, as this is one of the biggest threats to children's health and exacerbates health disparities. States should, therefore, put children's health concerns at the centre of their climate change adaptation and mitigation strategies".[59]

Applying this logic more generally, beyond the implementation of the right to health, the Director general of the WHO considers that "climate change should be incorporated into risk assessments, preparedness and response plans for health emergencies; climate resilience should be integrated into the building blocks of health systems".[60] Following this approach, the WHO has also created a department of public health, environmental and social determinants of health.[61]

Coordination means are also emerging in the context of instruments devoted to the protection of the environment. Several climate treaties such as the UNFCCC,[62] the Paris Agreement,[63] the Convention on Long-range Transboundary Air Pollution[64] and many other international environmental agreements include the protection of health as one of their main goals. The problem is that mechanisms of implementation of environmental agreements do not always reflect health concerns or take them sufficiently into account. In its report on *Climate Change 2001: Impacts, Adaptation, and Vulnerability*, the IPCC already included chapter 9 on "Human health". At that time there was limited evidence of climate change impacts on health, thus the report only suggested the use of a precautionary approach. The IPCC's position changed in the report *Climate Change 2014: Impacts, Adaptation, and Vulnerability* where the chapter on *Human Health: Impacts, Adaptation, and Co-Benefits* shows high confidence in the evidence regarding negative impacts of climate change on health and several epidemic outbreaks were linked to climate change. In its sixth assessment report *Climate Change 2022: Impacts, Adaptation and Vulnerability*, ways to adapt are considered in relation to high levels of human health, "ecosystem

59 CRC, General comment No 15 (2013) on the right of the child to the enjoyment of the highest attainable standard of health (Art. 24 of the Convention on the rights of the child), § 50.

60 WHO, Report of the Director General on "Health, environment and climate change", 9 April 2018, A71/10, § 32.

61 S. Negri, "A human rights approach to environmental health", at 25–41 in S. Negri (ed.), *Environmental health in international and EU law. Current challenges and legal responses, op. cit.*

62 Article 4 (f).

63 Preamble.

64 Article 1.

health"[65] and "planetary health".[66] The IPCC's approach has thus evolved by progressively addressing together the means of the fight against climate and health risks – these risks being now considered as intertwined.

4.3 Beginnings of Integration of the Two Risks: The Right to a Healthy and Sustainable Environment

Human rights law has recognised a "right to a healthy environment" which includes several international obligations related to these global risks. Health is the link between the environment and human rights, and provides an opportunity to demand compliance with obligations to combat climate change by taking into account its adverse health effects. Starting in the 1970s, several states have included in their national Constitutions a right to a healthy environment;[67] currently more than 80 per cent of states members of the United Nations (156 out of 193) legally recognise the right to a safe, clean, healthy and sustainable environment.[68] On the international plane, several regional instruments contain this right: the African Charter on Human and Peoples Rights provides that "all peoples shall have the right to a general satisfactory environment favorable to their development" (Article 24), the 1988 Additional Protocol to the American Convention on Human Rights states that "everyone shall have the right to live in a healthy environment" (Article 11, § 1), the Human Rights Declaration adopted by the Association of Southeast Asian Nations in November 2012 includes a "right to a safe, clean and sustainable environment" as an element of the right to an adequate standard of living (§ 28 (f)). Despite the silence of the Convention, the European Court of Human Rights has also introduced

65 Ecosystem health is defined as "a metaphor used to describe the condition of an ecosystem, by analogy with human health. Note that there is no universally accepted benchmark for a healthy ecosystem. Rather, the apparent health status of an ecosystem is judged on the ecosystem's resilience to change, with details depending upon which metrics (such as species richness and abundance) are employed in judging it and which societal aspirations are driving the assessment", IPCC, Sixth assessment report Climate Change 2022: Impacts, Adaptation and Vulnerability, at 7.

66 Planetary health is "a concept based on the understanding that human health and human civilisation depend on ecosystem health and the wise stewardship of ecosystems", *ibid.*

67 J.H. Knox, "Report of the Independent Expert on the issue of human rights obligations relating to the enjoyment of a safe, clean, healthy and sustainable environment", 24 December 2012, § 12.

68 "Right to a healthy environment: good practices - Report of the Special Rapporteur on the issue of human rights obligations relating to the enjoyment of a safe, clean, healthy and sustainable environment", 30 December 2019, A/HRC/43/53, § 13. See also <http://www.srenvironment.org/report/good-practices-in-implementing-the-right-to-a-healthy-environment-2020>.

the protection of a healthy environment as a guarantee required by the implementation of other rights, such as the rights to life, to respect for private and family life, and to property.[69] The Human Rights Council established a special rapporteur on human rights and the environment who clearly stressed the relationship between global risks related to climate change and health. In his 2020 report, he points to the need to address the "global nature emergency", in particular in order "not to make the same mistake with the risks posed by future pandemics, biodiversity loss and climate change".[70] The specific risks of climate damage have led to the creation by the Human Rights Council of a new special rapporteur on climate change who started to work in 2022.[71]

The right to a healthy environment includes among its substantive elements a safe climate and this is why its implementation may be informed by the obligations under the UNFCCC.[72] This link has been recognised by several international courts. In an advisory opinion of 15 November 2017 concerning the interpretation of Articles 1(1), 4(1) and 5(1) of the American Convention on Human Rights, the Interamerican Court of Human Rights stated that the term "jurisdiction" includes activities of states which have effects outside their territory, such as GHG emissions. The real test to be considered is the state's "effective control" of the activity. Thus, potentially victims living in another country can bring an action against the state concerned. The Court stated that the right to a healthy environment has both collective – including the interests of future generations – and individual aspects and that it includes the following main state obligations: to guarantee a healthy environment; to guarantee basic public services; to promote environmental protection and conservation; and to promote the improvement of the environment.[73] The African Commission on Human and People's rights also had the opportunity to specify the elements of this right, which includes states' obligations to use reasonable means at their disposal in order to prevent pollution and to guarantee a sustainable

---

69 See in particular ECtHR, *Budayeva and Others v. Russia*, 20 March 2008, application nos. 15339/02, 21166/02, 20058/02, 11673/02 and 15343/02 and ECtHR (Grand Chamber), *Guerra and others v. Italy*, 19 February 1998, application no 14967/89.

70 *Op. cit.*, § 81.

71 Resolution adopted by the Human Rights Council on 12 July 2019, A/HRC/RES/41/21.

72 Report of the Special Rapporteur on the issue of human rights obligations relating to the enjoyment of a safe, clean, healthy and sustainable environment, 15 July 2019, A/74/161, § 43.

73 M. Feria-Tinta, "CC as a HR issue: litigating CC in the inter-american system of HR and the UN Human rights committee", at 310 in I. Alogna, C. Bakker, J.-P. Gauci, *Climate change litigation: global perspectives*, Leiden, Boston, Brill Nijhoff, 2021, XXIV–544 p.

use of natural resources.[74] Climate change can have negative impacts on many human rights.[75] This is why the Office of the UN High Commissioner for Human Rights (OHCHR) has detailed the conditions for the implementation of states' obligations in relation to climate change: mitigating climate change by preventing impacts on human beings; ensuring that all people have the capacity to adapt; ensuring accountability and effective redress for damage to human beings; mobilising the maximum amount of resources; ensuring equity in climate action; and ensuring informed participation in decision-making.[76]

The first link between the protection of climate and of health against global risks is that the failure of states to take action in order to face climate change in accordance with their international obligations can be considered as a breach of the right to a safe and sustainable environment. Several domestic courts have ruled in this respect. While the claimants argued that Colombia's inaction to combat climate change threatened several of their rights including their right to health and the right to a healthy environment, the Supreme Court held that the "fundamental rights of life, health, the minimum subsistence, freedom, and human dignity are substantially linked and determined by the environment and the ecosystem".[77] The same kind of arguments are used in international litigation.[78] The United Nations Committee on the Rights of the Child, for example, has recognised that the rights to life, health and culture of several children were threatened by the climate inaction of states.[79]

The right to a healthy environment has finally been acknowledged, first at the universal level by the United Nations Human Rights Council in October 2021[80] and, subsequently, by the United Nations General Assembly on 28 July

74 African Commission on Human and Peoples' Rights, *Social and Economic Rights Centre (SERAC) and Centre for Economic and Social Rights (CESR) v. Nigeria*, decision of 27 October 2001, § 52–53.

75 Human Rights Committee, General comment No 36 on article 6: right to life (2018). According to the Committee, climate change is one of the greatest threats to the ability to exercise the right to life in the future.

76 Report of the Office of the United Nations High Commissioner for Human Rights on the relationship between climate change and human rights, A/HRC/10/61.

77 Supreme Court of Colombia, *Future Generations v. Ministry of the Environment and Others*, 5 April 2018, at 13. See also Lahore High Court, *Leghari v. Federation of Pakistan*, 25 January 2018, § 7.

78 C. Cournil, C. Perruso, "Réflexions sur l'humanisation des changements climatiques et la climatisation des droits de l'homme. Emergence et pertinence", *Revue des droits de l'homme*, 2018, no 14.

79 Committee on the Rights of the Child, *Sacchi, et al. v. Argentina et al.*, decisions adopted on 8 October 2021.

80 Human Rights Council, *The human right to a clean, healthy and sustainable environment*, resolution A/HRC/RES/48/13, 18 October 2021.

2022.[81] The official recognition of this right by the UN creates the opportunity to give concrete implementation to the Sustainable Development Goals by using a human rights perspective. "If we fail to employ a rights-based approach to achieving the Sustainable Development Goals, addressing the climate emergency, protecting the biosphere and detoxifying the global economy, today's children and future generations will live in an ecologically impoverished world, deprived of nature's critical contributions to human well-being, riven by deepening environmental injustices and ravaged by increasingly frequent pandemics".[82]

A second link between global risks related to climate change and pandemics is currently emerging: their interplay is starting to be used by litigants in order to combat activities favouring both risks. For example, an NGO filed an application against the United Kingdom to the European Court of Human Rights in 2022 aiming at challenging factory farming; it was however declared inadmissible by the Court at the end of the year.[83] The claimant alleged a breach of the right to life, the right not to be subjected to inhumane or degrading treatment and the right to respect for private and family life for failing to address the risks of the climate crisis, future pandemics and antibiotic resistance created by factory farming. It argued that the United Kingdom should consider the danger of agricultural methane emissions and the impact of soy feed consumption in factory farming as a key driver of deforestation in the Amazon. Integration of these global risks in a human rights perspective has thus had an impact on climate litigation by bringing forward future generations and ecosystems as rights holders and by introducing a future time frame.[84]

5 Conclusions

Global risks have long been identified and studied by researchers in hard sciences and several social sciences such as geography and sociology. They all agree on the identification of several broad categories of current global risks: economic, environmental, geopolitical, societal and technological. Their main

81 UNGA, *The human right to a clean, healthy and sustainable environment*, A/RES/76/300, 1 August 2022.

82 *Op. cit.*, § 79.

83 ECtHR, *Humane Being v. the United Kingdom*, 13 December 2022, application no. 36959/22.

84 S. Gloppen, C. Vallejo, "The climate crisis: litigation and economic, social and cultural rights", at 386, in J. Dugard, B. Porter, D. Ikawa, L. Chenwi (eds), *Research handbook on economic, social and cultural rights as human rights*, Cheltenham, Edward Elgar Publishing, 2020, XXVIII–422 p.

features consist in their level of indetermination, in their interconnectedness which generates a high level of complexity and in the seriousness and breadth of their effects. While domestic, regional and international courts are increasingly faced with these risks and while international legal fora address them on a regular basis, no legal definition has yet been proposed in order to identify them.

These risks evolve in a context of radical uncertainty where the precise consequences of their occurrence are unpredictable. The need to address this issue has led to the emergence through international law of precautionary approaches in order to define our relationship with Nature and to find a balance between the control that Man can exercise over Nature and the fact that he himself is a part of it.[85] Precaution expresses a disjunction between knowledge and technical power and a paradoxical emergency (which cannot be immediately defined) and creates a permanent obligation of risk objectivation.[86] Originally formulated in the Rio Declaration, the precautionary principle is now included in many international, regional and domestic legal rules. It allows uncertainty to be taken into account by acting to prevent damage. Uncertainty can have several degrees[87] and can concern the exact time of risk realisation, its effects, their localisation, the evolution of risk due to interactions with other risks etc.[88] Precaution covers particularly damage that occurs over time and that cannot be completely evaluated at a given time.[89]

Building on the current domestic and international practice, several elements can be pointed to in this regard which concern both the multiple origins and the complex legal effects of global risks. They have multiple causes linked mainly to lawful activities, including the actions and omissions of a plurality of actors having a potential global reach and they affect resources of common concern, thus producing a series of incidents of damage, the accumulation of which in space and time must be taken into account in order to evaluate the

85 D. Guével, "The precautionary principle. An instrument at the service of sustainable development", at 23 in M.B. Pillai, G. Ganapathy-Doré (eds), *Global commons. Issues, concerns and strategies*, Los Angeles, Sage, 2020, XIV–290 p.

86 Y. C. Zarka, "Considérations philosophiques sur le principe de précaution", *Revue de métaphysique et de morale*, 2012, at 483–489.

87 M.M. Mbengue, *Essai sur une théorie du risque en droit international public. L'anticipation du risque environnemental et sanitaire*, Paris, Pedone, 2009, at 15: uncertainty about the risk is sufficient to trigger a precautionary situation.

88 S. Cassella, "Les dynamiques de la précaution dans la lutte contre les changements climatiques", *Archives de philosophie du droit*, 2020, at 131–150.

89 J. Cazala, *Le principe de précaution en droit international*, Paris, Dalloz, 2006, 498 p.

total harm. While these criteria have been applied here specifically to the risks of climate change and pandemics, it seems they can also be used in order to study through a legal perspective other types of risks belonging to the other categories mentioned, including global financial crises,[90] cyber-risks[91] and transnational crimes such as terrorism.[92]

90 See for instance P. Dąbrowska-Kłosińska (ed.), *Essays on global safety governance: challenges and solutions*, Warsaw, Centre for Europe, University of Warsaw, 2015, XX–282 p.

91 See for instance M. Grange, A.-T. Norodom (eds), *Cyberattaques et droit international: problèmes choisis*, Paris, Pedone, 2019, 230 p., V. Radicevic, "Promoting Cyber Stability between States: OSCE Efforts to Reduce the Risks of Conflict Stemming from the Use of Information and Communication Technologies (ICTs) in the Context of Global and Regional Security", *Yearbook on the Organisation for Security and Co-operation in Europe (OSCE)*, 2017, at 201–212.

92 See for instance U.E. Siebert, "The Paradigm Shift in the Global Risk Society: From Criminal Law to Global Security Law - An Analysis of the Changing Limits of Crime Control", *Journal of Eastern-European criminal law*, 2016/1, at 14–27.

CHAPTER 2

The Role of International Law in Dealing with Global Risks

1 Introduction

International law has started to take the global risks of climate change and pandemics into account, first through general norms not specifically devoted to these issues, and then by elaborating specific legal instruments such as the UNFCCC or the IHR – the objects of the latter text being public health emergencies of international concern while an agreement on pandemics is currently being negotiated but has not yet been concluded. But the legal regime regulating these risks extends beyond the specific treaties devoted to them and includes various rules and obligations deriving from several other branches of international law which pursue various objectives (2). An efficient legal regime aimed at tackling global risks should mirror their peculiar features by articulating and coordinating action between all the relevant fields of international law and between the international and the domestic levels. Some mechanisms such as the integration principle are starting to be used in this way in order to mainstream global risks concerns in most state decision-making processes (3). While the action of several kinds of stakeholders is relevant in the fight against global risks, at present international law still focuses on state action by developing its due diligence obligations and, thus, its international responsibility for negligence in this regard (4).

2 Fragmentation of Legal Regimes Dealing with Global Risks

International law does not address each global risk through a specific and comprehensive legal regime. Some instruments are uniquely devoted to climate change or to epidemics, but these sets of norms are both complex and heterogeneous as they contain hard and soft law and need to be completed and implemented at other levels – regional and domestic (2.1). In order to derive a complete landscape these regimes must be complemented by external rules contained in instruments pursuing other objectives but which may strengthen states' obligations regarding global risks (2.2). Several other international legal regimes take into account states' measures aiming at combatting global risks

 | DOI:10.1163/9789004538702_004

only as exceptions to the rules they provide. But this rationale of exception, which has been elaborated for other types of contexts, does not seem to fit the specificities of global risks (2.3).

2.1 *The Complex Implementation of Legal Regimes Aiming at Preventing Global Risks*

As international law is not the only legal system involved in global risks, it addresses climate change and pandemics in a fragmented way. The first set of rules here examined aims at preventing the realisation of these risks by protecting the climate and health. Climate change rules are to be found in several treaties, but also in many soft-law instruments and rules relating to pandemics are present in the International Health Regulations and also in several soft-law instruments. Treaties addressing these global risks contain complex sets of provisions ranging from clearly mandatory clauses to mere recommendations. In order to know what is expected from states, they have to be read together and the implementation of these rules involves both regional law and domestic legal systems.

As regards the risk dimension of climate change, we focus here on the mitigation regime and not on adaptation which concerns the effects of the current realisations of the climate risk, even if there are obviously several links between the two kinds of obligations. First of all, several treaties have been concluded which protect specific components of the climate: this is, for instance, the case with treaties combatting pollution in order to preserve the atmosphere such as the 1979 Geneva Convention on Long-range Transboundary Air Pollution or with agreements on the protection of the ozone layer such as the 1985 Vienna Convention for the Protection of the Ozone Layer. The implementation of these older treaties contributes to the global legal regime dedicated to the fight against human-driven climate change.

The first legal text specifically devoted to this goal was the United Nations Framework Convention on Climate Change (UNFCCC) of 1992. Article 2 defines its ultimate objective which is "to achieve, in accordance with the relevant provisions of the Convention, stabilisation of greenhouse gas concentrations in the atmosphere at a level that would prevent dangerous anthropogenic interference with the climate system [...]". The main means of achieving this goal according to the convention are the reduction of greenhouse gas emissions and the enhancement of carbon sinks, i.e., reservoirs that absorb and store carbon. The UNFCCC includes a precautionary approach due to the very high uncertainty surrounding this risk and several seminal principles such as common but differentiated responsibilities. The convention has been completed by two protocols, the 1997 Kyoto Protocol[1] and the 2015 Paris Agreement. The Kyoto Protocol established specific GHG mitigation obligations for developed countries following a precise timetable, procedural obligations to report and review and a refined compliance system. It also created several market mechanisms for implementing these obligations.[2] The Paris Agreement, which has moved towards a different approach, is a good example of the complexity of the interplay between different kinds of provisions.[3] It introduces a new bottom-up approach by leaving wide discretion to states parties on the means to use in order to attain its reduction objective, through the elaboration of nationally determined contributions (NDCs), but it sets out a series of procedural obligations. They include the following: to prepare, communicate and pursue the successive NDCs which must represent a progression in mitigation (Article 4, §§ 2, 3 and 9); to provide sufficient information to other Parties in order to guarantee the transparency of the NDCs (Article 4, § 8); to account for its own NDCs (Article 4, § 13); specific obligations for States Parties which decide to act jointly (Article 4, §§ 15 to 17); to provide regular information on national GHG inventories and the information necessary to monitor progress in the implementation and achievement of a state's NDC (Article 13); financial obligations for developed states of assistance to developing-country parties (Article 9). These provisions include a web of obligations of result and of conduct while other clauses contain recommendations or incentives, thus creating a complex combination of hard and soft law.[4] Article 3 in particular lays down several standards that are necessary for implementing these obligations, as domestic courts have recognised;[5] it thus creates normative expectations.[6] Some authors consider that the Paris Agreement thus establishes several interactions between an international incentive regime and strong domestic policies, between mandatory procedural obligations and normative expectations

1 This Protocol has created markets for quantified emissions allowances for developed states and its obligations were extended to 2020, but many states gradually withdrew from it.

2 D. Bodansky, J. Brunnée, L. Rajamani, *International climate change law*, Oxford University Press, 2017, at 160 *et seq.*

3 On this issue see D. Bodansky, "The legal character of the Paris Agreement", *RECIEL*, 2016/2, at 142.

4 D. Bodansky, J. Brunnée, L. Rajamani, *International climate change law*, *op. cit.*, at 213.

5 See for instance Mexico, Eleventh Collegiate Court of the First Circuit in Administrative Matters, *Greenpeace v. Instituto Nacional de Ecología y Cambio Climático and Others*, 21 September 2021.

6 L. Rajamani, "Innovation and Experimentation in the International Climate Change Regime", *Collected Courses of the Hague Academy of International Law*, vol. 404, 2020, at 187–191.

guided by due diligence, between states and non-state actors.[7] Moreover, the COP24 has adopted in 2018 the Paris Rulebook which contains rules establishing procedures and standards for the implementation of the Paris Agreement obligations including, for example, the list of information that has to be provided on NDCs. These rules have been adopted in the form of soft law but they are a necessary tool for interpreting and setting the scope of the Parties' obligations. The Paris Agreement also creates a compliance committee of experts which can act in connection with the implementation of certain procedural obligations.

This international framework clearly designates domestic law – or regional law if collective action is taken, such as within the European Union – as the main level of action for climate change mitigation and attributes to states parties the responsibility for controlling private actors under their jurisdiction in order to attain the mitigation objective.

Turning to health risks, in order to prevent the emergence of epidemics, the WHO in 1951 adopted the International Health Regulations (IHR),[8] the first single legal regime for the surveillance and control of "quarantine diseases" that was binding on all its members. The IHR replaced all sanitary conventions adopted by Member States in the first half of the 20th century. Despite improvements and updates in 1969, 1973 and 1981, the Regulations have not fulfilled their main purpose for several reasons. To address these shortcomings, a major revision took place in 2005: expertise became the main legitimising factor (depoliticisation) to be taken into account in taking sanitary measures; the WHO can now gather information from a variety of sources well beyond states' official authorities and the process is opened up to all public health emergencies of international concern beside any specific list of diseases. The IHR were thus transformed into a global alert and response system.

Their aim is to delegate significant powers to the Director General of the WHO and to impose a set of demanding obligations on States Parties, while leaving them the discretion to adopt the national health measures necessary to prevent and control epidemics on their territory and to organise their "national focal points". They contain three types of state obligations: to develop, strengthen and maintain essential capacities for surveillance of, preparedness for and response to public health risks; obligations of due diligence in cooperating with other states and with the WHO for the sharing of information and the implementation of health measures; and the adoption of national public health measures based on necessity, proportionality, scientific evidence and

7 L. Rajamani, *ibid.*, at 189.

8 Until 1969 they were known as the "International sanitary regulations".

risk assessment. Here too, the articulation with the domestic – or regional – implementation of these obligations is crucial: the Director General of the WHO has the power to declare a public health emergency of international concern on the advice of a scientific committee, this declaration triggering his/her power to recommend to states parties the domestic health measures that have to be taken. Here again, even if the recommendations are not mandatory, the IHR provide for a series of standards useful for the evaluation of the implementation of the states' obligations: they set criteria for the obligation of notification, an algorithm helping to determine whether a state is facing a health emergency, a deadline for instituting national monitoring capacities ... [9] The persistent inefficiency of the IHR often pointed to[10] – including during the COVID-19 pandemic[11] – pertains to the inadequacy of the majority of national health systems' response to health emergencies and to the insufficient implementation of the WHO's recommendations. According to Article 43, states can choose to deviate from the Director General's recommendations but, in this case, they have to justify their decision. The main difficulty is that the WHO does not have the capacity to control or to sanction these deviations.

The very definition of global risk, as we have seen, implies that several kinds of actors may be at the origin of its realisation, including by not having employed the means to prevent it. Among these we can find international organisations, but at the moment it seems difficult to succeed in imposing them obligations to prevent and respond to the emergence of global risks. The international legal regime on climate change does not specifically address the issue of the participation of international organisations in its prevention, even if the United Nations, for example, – specifically through UNEP – assume the functions of sharing research knowledge and recommendations on this issue, monitoring the progress of states in achieving common goals and facilitating the inclusion of non-state actors. The situation is rather different concerning the global risk of pandemics. The analysis of this issue depends on the subject to which the organisation has an obligation. Sometimes it is indeed possible to identify obligations of the organisation to its member states or its agents, which are therefore mostly within its own legal order. It is much more difficult to identify international obligations to third parties and, in particular,

9 G. Rodier, "Le Règlement sanitaire international révisé", at 73 in SFDI, *La responsabilité de protéger*, Paris, Pedone, 2008, 358 p.

10 G.L. Burci, "The Legal Response to Pandemics", *Journal of International Humanitarian Legal Studies*, 2020/1, at 8.

11 See the Report of the Review Committee on the Functioning of the International Health Regulations (2005) during the COVID-19 response, <https://www.who.int/publications/m/item/a74-9-who-s-work-in-health-emergencies>.

private persons.[12] With regard to the relations of Member States with the WHO, it is possible to look for the organisation's obligations within the International Health Regulations. Its essential function in this context is to gather health information, to ensure its circulation as quickly as possible, to process it in order to declare a possible health emergency of international concern and to draw up recommendations for the Member States. Few more specific obligations can be identified in relation to this coordination and assessment role; they relate mainly to monitoring the health situation (Article 5) and communicating the information obtained (Article 11). Articles 9 and 10 also allow the WHO to initiate a verification procedure in a Member State even before it reports a new pathogen. The language used in these texts is not very precise and seems to refer more to an empowerment for the WHO in the event that it has gathered information from non-state sources. In the case of COVID-19, the WHO set up a joint mission with China in 2020 to investigate the transmissibility of the virus, the severity of the disease and the impact of the initial measures taken. It is questionable whether it fulfilled its obligations in this way.[13] The right to health also appears to be difficult to enforce against the WHO as that body is not a party to the main treaties that enshrine the right. The Committee on Economic, Social and Cultural Rights has nonetheless indicated that international organisations also have responsibilities for health protection, but without referring to specific obligations.[14] Most organisations have very few normative powers. Nevertheless, their actions have long had effects on private actors outside the mediation of the state, although this cannot be explained solely in terms of the functionalist perspective of implicit powers. The classical model of their authority does not allow for the damaging effects that can arise when they have "public authority" over actors other than their member states.[15] Yet the negligence of the WHO has already been noted, notably during the Ebola epidemic in 2014.[16] In these circumstances, rather than international responsibility for internationally wrongful acts, it is often accountability

12 See M. Hartwig, "International Organisations or Institutions, Responsibility and Liability", *MPEPIL*, § 3.

13 See, for instance, M.A. Becker, "Do we need an international commission of inquiry for COVID-19?", *EJIL: Talk!*, 18 May 2020.

14 CESCR, General Comment No 14 (2000), *op. cit.*, § 42.

15 J. Klabbers, "The EJIL foreword: The Transformation of International Organisations Law", *EJIL*, 2015/1, at 9.

16 M. Eccleston-Turner, S. McArdle, R. Upshur, "Accountability, International Law, and the World Health Organisation: A need for Reform?", *Global Health Governance*, 2017, at 27–40.

mechanisms that promote the development of international organisations' obligations by reference to their diligence.[17]

Three major flaws can be observed in these legal regimes aimed at preventing the global risks linked to climate change and to pandemics. First, these risks and the measures taken in order to face them both have huge consequences for several other legally protected interests: human rights, economy, trade, intellectual property rights, investment, transport, migration ... Ignoring these interactions by focusing only on a specific risk limits the efficiency of the international and national action of the different stakeholders. Second, both regimes are affected by the prisoner's dilemma: general cooperation is the only means of avoiding global risks in the long term but the expectation of short-term individual gains tends to favour unilateral action. Thus, facing the spread of a contagious disease, states tend to close borders, to prohibit exports of health products, to produce and keep vaccines for domestic consumption etc. In the fight against climate change, states also often defer mitigating measures on the basis that other states have taken insufficient action and in order to maintain the competitiveness of their companies. The prisoner's dilemma is worsened by the global dimension of these risks: all states have to face them but they do not have the same vulnerability to these risks at the same moment. Third and last, the efficiency of these legal regimes is hindered both by the interplay between their different kinds of rules (of hard and of soft law) and by the interaction between the international, regional and domestic levels for their implementation. However, they should also be read in conjunction with international legal regimes that follow another purpose.

2.2 *Interactions with Other International Legal Regimes*

Legal regimes devoted to the prevention of and response to global risks are complemented by norms included in other fields which can be relevant for this purpose by strengthening the effects of their provisions. The International Law Commission has stressed the complementarity of various international law regimes in its *Articles on the protection of persons in the event of disasters* by mentioning "the overall panoply of instruments and arrangements that exist at the international level in the context of disaster relief assistance, as well as disaster risk reduction".[18] Even if this text mainly covers the response to disasters which have already occurred, it also addresses the reduction of risks of a "calamitous event or series of events resulting in widespread loss of life,

17 G. Hafner, "Accountability of International Organisations", ASIL *Proceedings of the Annual Meeting*, 2003, at 236–240.

18 Commentary on article 2, § 5.

great human suffering and distress, mass displacement, or large-scale material or environmental damage, thereby seriously disrupting the functioning of society";[19] this description seems possibly to cover global risks as defined here and thus the content of the Articles could be worth taking into account.

A first example concerns the interplay between climate law and the law of the sea. Several provisions of the United Nations Convention on the Law of the Sea (UNCLOS) may be articulated with international climate law in order to contribute to the fight against climate change – as long as both sets of legal rules are binding on specific states. The first question to be resolved is whether emissions of GHG into the atmosphere can be included among the causes of pollution of the marine environment that states must combat in accordance with UNCLOS. In view of the definition given in Article 1, § 4,[20] and of the findings established by the IPCC reports,[21] it seems that these may indeed correspond to the indirect human introduction into the marine environment of energy likely to produce harmful effects on the environment. This interpretation is confirmed by Article 212 of UNCLOS which clearly refers to the adoption by states of international rules and standards to "prevent, reduce and control" pollution from atmospheric sources.[22]

---

19 Article 3 a).

20 "'Pollution of the marine environment' means the introduction by man, directly or indirectly, of substances or energy into the marine environment, including estuaries, which results or is likely to result in such deleterious effects as harm to living resources and marine life, hazards to human health, hindrance to marine activities, including fishing and other legitimate uses of the sea, impairment of quality for use of sea water and reduction of amenities". See also G. Xue, "Climate Change Challenges and the Law of the Sea Responses", at 574 in O.C. Ruppel, C. Roschmann, K. Ruppel-Schlichting (eds), *Climate Change: International Law and Global Governance, Volume I: Legal Responses and Global Responsibility*, Baden Baden, Nomos, 2013, 1018 p.

21 IPCC, "2019 Special Report on the Ocean and Cryosphere in a Changing Climate", Chapter 1 - Framing and Context of the Report.

22 "Pollution from or through the atmosphere

1. States shall adopt laws and regulations to prevent, reduce and control pollution of the marine environment from or through the atmosphere, applicable to the air space under their sovereignty and to vessels flying their flag or vessels or aircraft of their registry, taking into account internationally agreed rules, standards and recommended practices and procedures and the safety of air navigation.
2. States shall take other measures as may be necessary to prevent, reduce and control such pollution.
3. States, acting especially through competent international organisations or diplomatic conference, shall endeavour to establish global and regional rules, standards and recommended practices and procedures to prevent, reduce and control such pollution".

Turning to the obligations to protect the marine environment as provided for in the law of the sea, Article 192 of UNCLOS sets out a general obligation in this respect, which may be subdivided into several obligations of diligence, contained in particular in Articles 194 and 195. Following recent case law,[23] this general obligation can be interpreted as including obligations to mitigate climate change – the protection of the marine environment being aimed at future damage. The fight against GHG emissions that could lead to harmful climate change may thus fall under Article 194, § 2,[24] of UNCLOS, which constitutes a specific application of the customary "no harm rule". By referring to activities under the "jurisdiction" or "control" of states, Article 194 of UNCLOS assumes an extraterritorial scope which fits particularly well with the logic of the law of the sea but which also corresponds to the decisions of the ICJ which broaden the scope of the no harm rule[25] and of the duty of prevention.[26] The law of the sea is thus a specific area in which the climate obligations of states apply, and, in reverse, the provisions of UNCLOS can be read against those of the Paris Agreement. Articles 194 and 207 of UNCLOS refer to rules and standards from other areas of international law and thus potentially to the Paris Agreement in the context of marine environmental protection. The interaction of these legal regimes is likely to make the fight against climate change more effective, mainly through the interpretation of states' due diligence obligations.[27]

Turning to the global risk of pandemics, the legal regime mainly instituted by the International Health Regulations can also be complemented by other types of international obligations of states. The main driver of the multiplication and diversification of these obligations is human rights law, at least it has been since the emergence of the right to health. First mentioned in the WHO

23 PCA, *The South China Sea Arbitration* (*The Republic of Philippines v. The People's Republic of China*), award, 12 July 2016, § 941. See also N. Oral, "International law as an adaptation measure to sea-level rise and its impacts on islands and offshore features", *The International Journal of Marine and Coastal Law*, 2019, at 415–439.

24 "States shall take all measures necessary to ensure that activities under their jurisdiction or control are so conducted as not to cause damage by pollution to other States and their environment, and that pollution arising from incidents or activities under their jurisdiction or control does not spread beyond the areas where they exercise sovereign rights in accordance with this Convention".

25 ICJ, *Legality of the Threat or Use of Nuclear Weapons*, advisory opinion, 8 July 1996, § 29.

26 According to the International Court of Justice, "A State is thus obliged to use all the means at its disposal in order to avoid activities which take place in its territory, or in any area under its jurisdiction, causing significant damage to the environment of another State", *Pulp Mills on the River Uruguay* (*Argentina v. Uruguay*), judgment, 20 April 2010, § 101.

27 See *infra*, Chapter 2, 4.

Constitution, the right to health has been included in several human rights treaties of universal,[28] sectoral[29] and regional[30] scope and is covered by more than 110 domestic constitutions.[31] Multiple health obligations specifically devoted to the prevention of epidemics arise from the right to health as set out in human rights treaties and as enshrined in the practice of international courts and quasi-judicial bodies.

In a general comment, the UN Committee on Economic, Social and Cultural Rights has developed its interpretation of Article 12 of the International Covenant on Civil and Political Rights (ICCPR). Among core minimum obligations related to the right to health, states have "to take measures to prevent, treat and control epidemic and endemic diseases".[32] Having a minimum health care system for the prevention of contagious diseases is considered an obligation of result.[33] But on other aspects, the right to health broadly meets the principle of progressivity, which means that its obligations must be implemented in the long run by states parties. This fact does not preclude states from taking ongoing measures whose implementation can be assessed at a given time. For example, "the right to treatment includes the creation of a system of urgent medical care in cases of accidents, epidemics and similar health hazards, and the provision of disaster relief and humanitarian assistance in emergency situations".[34] According to this interpretation by the Committee on Economic, Social and Cultural Rights, the allocation of an inadequate budget for setting up a rapid response system for health emergencies could constitute a violation of state obligations related to the right to health.[35] Two characteristics of this right tend to strengthen the prevention of pandemics. First, the right

28 Most notably in article 12 of the ICCPR.

29 E.g., Article 24 of the International Convention on the Rights of the Child and Article 5 of the International Convention on the Elimination of All Forms of Racial Discrimination.

30 Article 16 of the African Charter on Human and Peoples' Rights, Article 10 of the Additional Protocol to the American Convention on Human Rights in the Area of Economic, Social and Cultural Rights, Article 11 of the European Social Charter.

31 OHCHR, "The right to health", Fact sheet no 31, <https://www.ohchr.org/sites/default/files/Documents/Publications/Factsheet31.pdf>.

32 CESCR, General Comment No 14 (2000), *op. cit.*, § 44.

33 R. Pisillo Mazzeschi, "Responsabilité de l'État pour violation des obligations positives relatives aux droits de l'Homme", *Collected Courses of The Hague Academy of International Law*, 2008, vol. 333, at 339.

34 CESCR, General Comment No 14 (2000), *op. cit.*, § 16.

35 CESCR, *ibid.*, § 52. On this issue see O. De Schutter, "Public budget analysis for the realisation of economic, social and cultural rights: conceptual framework and practical implementation", at 527, in K.G. Young, *The future of economic and social rights*, Cambridge, CUP, 2019.

to health is given extraterritorial scope because states have an obligation to prevent its violation outside their territory and to take it into account during the conclusion and implementation of their international agreements.[36] They also have to ensure that their decisions within the framework of international organisations of which they are members "take due account of the right to health".[37] Second, the right to health is considered as both an individual and a collective right that can be invoked before the courts. The African Commission on Human and Peoples' Rights, for example, declared that Nigeria had violated the Ogoni people's right to health and ordered specific collective remedies in this respect.[38] These examples show that the legal regime of prevention of the global risks related to climate change and to pandemics is rather complex because it results from the interplay of very different sets of international norms that follow their own purpose and logic.

2.3 *The Shortcomings of the Rationale of Exception*

A last set of much more heterogeneous international rules takes into consideration the measures aimed at fighting global risks as mere exceptions to the obligations they contain and which are affected by them.[39] This is the case with several regimes pertaining to international economic law or even to human rights law.[40] This rationale of exception was not imagined in a context of global risks and is not the appropriate way to deal with them. This section focuses on the topical field of international economic law, more precisely on international trade law and on foreign investment law. Global risks can *a priori* be addressed in these two legal regimes under consideration by different means, the common feature of which is that they are based on the logic of the exception. According to one author, "[t]he term 'exception' is used in international legal discourse to refer to a wide variety of techniques that provide

36 CESCR, *ibid.*, § 39.

37 CESCR, *ibid.*

38 African Commission on Human and People's Rights, *Social and economic rights action centre and Centre for economic and social rights v. Nigeria*, 13–27 October 2001, No 155/96. On the collective dimension of this right see T. Gründler, "L'effectivité du droit à la protection de la santé", *Revue générale de droit médical*, 2010, special issue, at 83–100.

39 This issue is discussed in J.E. Viñuales, *Foreign investment and the environment in international law*, Cambridge University Press, 2012, XLVIII–424 p. and in P. Sands, J. Peel, A. Fabra Aguilar, R. Mckenzie, *Principles of international environmental law*, Cambridge University Press, 2018, LXVIII–968 p.

40 Human rights law is rather specific because it also includes the protection of health and of the environment under the form of subjective rights. In the context of global risks, the issue is thus to keep the balance between the exercise of some human rights and the protection of other rights threatened by global risks.

special legal treatment to certain situations otherwise governed by a general rule".[41] Some of these mechanisms are "first-degree norms", which provide both an obligation and its limits in certain circumstances; others are "second-degree norms", which do not contain obligations but are intended solely to restrict the scope of other norms (such as derogations or general exceptions); and still others take the form of justifications for a breach of international law (such as necessity). Although there are a number of differences between these three types of rules, they are examined together here because they are all used as a basis for the non-implementation of the international obligations under consideration and follow a very similar logic, that of exception.

Most trade agreements provide for a number of specific and general exceptions that may be relevant to state measures aiming at preventing global risks. With regard to the WTO agreements, specific exceptions include GATT Article XI, § 2, a) on the elimination of quantitative restrictions.[42] The general exception of GATT Article XX can also be mentioned.[43] Article IX of the WTO Agreement moreover provides for the possibility of requesting a temporary waiver in exceptional circumstances. Other agreements are also concerned with measures protecting health or the environment, and in particular Article 2.2 of the Agreement on the Application of Sanitary and Phytosanitary Measures ("SPS" Agreement).[44] Its interpretation follows the same logic as that of Article XX of the GATT.

A number of investment protection agreements contain second-tier standards in the form of safeguard clauses to exclude the applicability of their

41 J.-E. Viñuales, "Seven ways of escaping a rule. Of exceptions and their avatars in international law", at 67–78, in L. Bartels, F. Paddeu (eds), *Exceptions in International Law*, Oxford University Press, 2020, VI–416 p.

42 "The provisions of paragraph 1 of this Article shall not extend to the following:
(a) Export prohibitions or restrictions temporarily applied to prevent or relieve critical shortages of foodstuffs or other products essential to the exporting contracting party".

43 "Subject to the requirement that such measures are not applied in a manner which would constitute a means of arbitrary or unjustifiable discrimination between countries where the same conditions prevail, or a disguised restriction on international trade, nothing in this Agreement shall be construed to prevent the adoption or enforcement by any contracting party of measures: …
(b) necessary to protect human, animal or plant life or health; …
(g) relating to the conservation of exhaustible natural resources if such measures are made effective in conjunction with restrictions on domestic production or consumption …".

44 "Members shall ensure that any sanitary or phytosanitary measure is applied only to the extent necessary to protect human, animal or plant life or health, is based on scientific principles and is not maintained without sufficient scientific evidence, except as provided for in paragraph 7 of Article 5".

provisions in certain exceptional circumstances, including to protect public health and the environment.[45] These necessity clauses are present in only about 30 bilateral investment treaties (BITS), as well as in the Canadian model BIT. In fairly recent treaties general exception clauses can be found which are modelled on Article XX of the GATT and interpreted in the same way, such as Article 8(3) of the United States model BIT. In the absence of express clauses, states may also attempt to justify their health or climate measures on the basis of customary necessity as codified by the International Law Commission (ILC) in the *Articles on state responsibility for internationally wrongful acts* (ARSIWA); this defence was largely used, for example. in the argentinean litigation.[46] Finally, this type of measure can be analysed through the doctrine of police powers, which preserves the right of states to take non-discriminatory measures in the general interest in accordance with due process of law. In this respect, Annex 8-A of the CETA expressly mentions the objective of protecting health and the environment.[47]

The imbalance between economic interests and protection against global risks at the international level is accentuated by the legal regime that is supposed to protect health and the climate. The International Health Regulations, for example, the purpose of which is to prevent and respond to epidemics, also take into account the interest of preserving trade.[48] In the same vein, article 3 § 5, of the UNFCCC affirms that "[t]he Parties should cooperate to promote a supportive and open international economic system that would lead to sustainable economic growth and development in all Parties, particularly developing country Parties, thus enabling them better to address the problems of climate change. Measures taken to combat climate change, including unilateral ones, should not constitute a means of arbitrary or unjustifiable discrimination or

45 C. Henckels, "Scope limitation or affirmative defence? The purpose and role of investment treaty exception clauses", at 364, in L. Bartels, F. Paddeu, (eds), *Exceptions in International Law*, Oxford University Press, 2020, VI–416 p.

46 This expression refers to the litigation brought against Argentina before arbitral tribunals by foreign investors after this state's sovereign default in the early 2000s. See for instance T.M. Araya, "A Decade of Sovereign Debt Litigation: Lessons from the *NML v Argentina* Case and the Road Ahead", *Business Law International*, 2016/2, at 83–101.

47 "3. For greater certainty, except in the rare circumstance when the impact of a measure or series of measures is so severe in light of its purpose that it appears manifestly excessive, non-discriminatory measures of a Party that are designed and applied to protect legitimate public welfare objectives, such as health, safety and the environment, do not constitute indirect expropriations".

48 See article 2: "The purpose and scope of these Regulations are to prevent, protect against, control and provide a public health response to the international spread of disease in ways that are commensurate with and restricted to public health risks, and which avoid unnecessary interference with international traffic and trade".

a disguised restriction on international trade". According to some authors, "[i]nternational economic law today prioritises trade and investment by treating values like health and environmental protection as 'exceptions'. This commerce-first stance is then mirrored in instruments on public health".[49]

However, this logic of exception responds very imperfectly to the global risks of pandemics and climate change for at least three reasons. First, these risks are characterised by a complex relationship between global and local necessity. Not all health and environmental exceptions are based on the existence of exceptional circumstances or a situation of emergency but, insofar as they lead to the failure of states' economic obligations, they require that states pursue a legitimate and clearly identified objective and that their measures are strictly adapted to it. Here, the objective of states is to protect their population and the international community from the risks linked to climate change and to pandemics, and therefore to respond to situations of necessity that must be precisely identified. In this type of context, most of the time, exceptions are envisaged in the various economic instruments (and in customary law as regards state of necessity) as means available to one or more states facing exceptional circumstances in order to prevent the strict observance of their obligations from giving rise to excessive social cost.[50] However, the specificity of climate change and of pandemics such as COVID-19 is that they affect all states almost simultaneously, with variable intensity according to different phases, different regions and different degrees of vulnerability. These risks are long-term in nature. This makes it difficult to grasp the specificity of the situation in a given state as is required by exceptions, and even raises doubts about the level of consideration given to the risk, which may be local or global.[51]

At the global level, it is relatively easy to admit the seriousness of the effects of these global risks, since they have already caused serious damage and continue to produce largely unpredictable effects. These serious threats to the essential interests of states are also evident as they affect the very survival of their populations. The WTO Appellate Body, for instance, has clearly recognised the importance of the objectives of protecting public health and the environment and the right of Member States to take measures to achieve

49 J. Arato, K. Claussen, J. Benton Heath, "The Perils of Pandemic Exceptionalism", *AJIL*, 2020, at 636.

50 On this notion see S. Cassella, *La nécessité en droit international. De l'état de nécessité aux situations de nécessité*, Leiden, Brill Nijhoff, 2011, at 87.

51 M. Samson, "L'Organisation mondiale du commerce: un forum approprié pour la protection de la santé publique?", in M. Kohen, D. Bentolila (eds), *Mélanges en l'honneur du professeur Jean-Michel Jacquet: le droit des rapports internationaux économiques et privés*, Paris, LexisNexis, 2013, XXVI–564 p.

them,[52] a right enshrined in Article 2(1) of the SPS Agreement. Similarly, arbitral tribunals have insisted on the right of states to adopt regulations in pursuit of these essential interests.[53]

The assessment of the reality of risks allowing the adoption of restrictive measures is, however, more complex in this context of global risks. It is well established in international law that a state does not have to wait for the realisation of the risk to adopt necessity measures. It has only to demonstrate that the risk it faces is imminent.[54] Assessing the multiplicity of successive health measures adopted by states in the case of a pandemic is difficult, because they are not dealing with a one-off risk established once and for all, but rather with a subset of risks that differ according to the specific phase under examination. These phases materialise, for example, within pandemics, with epidemic rebounds. While the situation is considered to be "under control" locally in some states, others still face critical situations, which makes the analysis at the global and local levels quite different. How is it possible to take into account, with regard to a state where the situation is temporarily under control, the risk of a variant spreading from the other side of the world? What level of anticipation of risk elsewhere can be accepted to justify the adoption of exceptional measures by each state? The same is true for climate change measures: specific extreme climate events affect the different regions of the World rather unevenly even if the whole of the international community is simultaneously concerned with climate change negative effects.

Second, it is difficult to draw a temporal delimitation of the exceptional situation. Health and environmental exceptions in the economic sphere are most often envisaged as temporary, but in all cases it must be possible to verify that states' measures are appropriate to the legitimate objective pursued. This requires being able to define, in temporal terms, the beginning and the end of the exceptional situation. Moreover, certain safeguard clauses and the customary state of necessity[55] clearly require that exceptional measures cease as soon as the critical situation is no longer present. Courts do not hesitate to define

52 See for instance Appellate Body, *European Communities—Measures Affecting Asbestos and Products Containing Asbestos*, 12 March 2001, WT/DS135/AB/R, § 168–172.

53 See for instance *Philip Morris Brands SARL, Philip Morris Products SA v Uruguay*, award, 8 July 2016, no ARB/10/7, § 287.

54 ICJ, *Gabčíkovo-Nagymaros Project (Hungary/Slovakia)*, Judgment, 25 September 1997, at 42.

55 J. Crawford, *Les articles de la C.D.I. sur la responsabilité de l'État. Introduction, texte et commentaires*, Paris, Pedone, 2003, at 221.

these temporal phases precisely.[56] But the boundaries between normality and exception are not clear in the case of global risks. While the beginning and the end of short-term and intense sub-events – such as a pandemic rebound or a severe climate event – may be identified, these global risks are latent and extend in the long term. It is even difficult to imagine what the criteria for their extinction could be: the limitation of global warming to a specific degree at a specific point in time? The transformation of a pandemic into a seasonal illness? This is all the more evident, given that many of the measures needed to face global risks are likely to extend beyond the eventual declaration of the end of an emergency phase because prevention is paramount; however, this possibility is not foreseen by exceptions in the legal regimes under consideration here.

Third, the contribution of states to the situation of necessity must be taken into account. The overall risks of climate change and epidemics are characterised by multiple acts and omissions that cause the final damage. The negligence of a large number of states has contributed to the current state of affairs as regards climate change and the COVID-19 pandemic, for instance. These different types of negligence that have at least contributed to the aggravation of the situation are likely to be taken into account with regard to the implementation of different health exceptions relevant in international economic law. Yet, at least for some states, it is very likely that their negligence can be analysed as a substantial contribution to the occurrence of their own situation of need – or even of the global situation for some. This kind of negligence is taken into account for the evaluation of the necessity defence (Article 25 of the ARSIWA) and contributory negligence could also be a contextual element that would most likely weigh, for example, in an arbitral tribunal's assessment of a state's use of its police powers in the environment and public health fields.[57] In conclusion, the rationale of exception does not suit the fight against global risks, above all because it cannot justify long-term and progressive measures which are crucial in this context.

56 *LG & E Energy Corp. and others v Argentina*, Decision on Liability, 3 October 2006, no ARB/02/1, § 227–261.

57 A. de Nanteuil, *International Investment Law*, Cheltenham, UK: Edward Elgar Publishing Limited, 2020, at 362.

3 The Integration Principle and the Links Created through Mainstreaming

Confronted with environmental global challenges, international law has developed the integration principle which has been included in several legal instruments and has been transposed into other fields. This principle is perfectly suited to global risks because it takes into account their pervasive nature and the ways in which they interact with several other state interests (3.1). The integration principles advocates for mainstreaming global risks concerns into state actions following two perspectives. First, this integrative approach should be implemented through international state action by taking into account the foreseeable impacts on climate change and on pandemics (3.2). Second, states should mainstream global risks concerns into their various domestic public policies through several tools such as impact assessments that can be evaluated by international institutions (3.3).

3.1 *The Integration Principle and Global Risks*

Environmental law has long recognised the role of the "integration principle", for instance through the notion of sustainable development. This notion was formulated in a general way in Principle 4 of the Rio Declaration: "[i]n order to achieve sustainable development, environmental protection shall constitute an integral part of the development process and cannot be considered in isolation from it". Since then, it has been incorporated into several treaties and in the practice of international bodies and institutions.[58] This principle is also present in the legal regimes related to the global risks of climate change and of epidemics. Article 3, § 4, of the UNFCCC establishes that "[i]n their actions to achieve the objective of the Convention and to implement its provisions, the Parties shall be guided, inter alia, by the following: … 4. The Parties have a right to, and should, promote sustainable development. Policies and measures to protect the climate system against human-induced change should be appropriate for the specific conditions of each Party and should be integrated with national development programmes, taking into account that economic development is essential for adopting measures to address climate change". This norm refers to the domestic effects of the integration principle,[59] which requires the inclusion of preventive climate measures in all national policies.

58 See A. Nollkaemper, "Three Conceptions of the Integration Principle in International Environmental Law", at 24 in A. Lenschow (ed.), *Environmental Policy Integration. Greening Sectoral Policies in Europe*, London, Routledge, 2001, 256 p.

59 See *infra*, Chapter 2, 3.

The same principle is implicit also in the international regimes protecting health. In its General Comment no 14, the Committee on Economic, Social and Cultural Rights affirmed that the right to health must be taken into account by states parties in all their international activities, including the conclusion of international agreements.[60] This applies also to the protection of the right to health from epidemics. In this regard, the Committee emphasises the international effects of the integration principle and the necessity of considering together the policies related to the different determinants of health.[61] In these cases, integration is understood as a principle that requires consideration of global risks in other fields where states' and other actors' actions could be relevant for these risks. André Nollkaemper considers that it covers two aspects: a procedural one which requires consideration of these interests in all decision-making and a substantive one which requires a balancing of two conflicting standards in a specific case.[62]

The main reason for applying the integration principle to global risks is that they can be considered to relate to public goods or "common concerns of humankind".[63] Public goods can be defined as goods that are non-excludable (no one can be prevented from using them) and non-rivalrous (the use by some people does not reduce the availability to the others). Neither the climate nor health can currently be considered as a pure public good, but some authors – mainly economists – refer to them as "global public goods" because they are goods necessary for Humankind and which are threatened mainly by the effects of globalisation.[64] The UNPD often refers to global public goods, among which health can be found.[65] International law takes this aspect into account, in particular by protecting these goods through *erga omnes* obligations and through the notion of "common concern of Humankind" which is based on the vital nature of a good for humanity, on its global character and therefore on the importance of the universality of cooperation for its conservation, and

60 CESCR, General Comment No 14 (2000), *op. cit.*, § 39.

61 CESCR, *ibid.*, § 16.

62 A. Nollkaemper, "Three Conceptions of the Integration Principle in International Environmental Law", *op. cit.*, at 30.

63 See *infra*, Chapter 4, 2.2.

64 N. Tanti-Hardouin, "La santé, bien public mondial? Le point de vue de l'économiste", at 169, in R. Mehdi, S. Maljean-Dubois (eds), *La société internationale et les grandes pandémies*, Paris, Pedone, 2007, 222 p.

65 M. Delmas-Marty, *Vers une communauté de valeurs?*, Paris, Editions du Seuil, 2011, at 351. See also B. Boidin, "Bien public mondial (approche économique)", at 94 in M. Cornu, F. Orsi, J. Rochfeld (eds), *Dictionnaire des biens communs*, Paris, PUF, 2017, XXVIII–1240 p.

on the fact of its being under threat of very serious and potentially irreversible damage.[66] This was used notably by the General Assembly of the United Nations in its resolution 43/53 in relation to the climate.[67] The Paris Agreement confirmed this qualification in its preamble and linked this concern to other human rights. This notion is present in several other treaties,[68] but without thus far generating a specific legal regime. While the Additional Protocol to the American Convention on Human Rights in the area of Economic, Social and Cultural Rights, in Article 10, § 2, takes health into account as a "public good",[69] it seems that international law more often considers it as a common concern.[70] Even if it does not entail any specific obligation, this notion nevertheless produces some legal effects that are examined in the last chapter of this book.[71] The notion of common concern of humankind also has several consequences in terms of "anticipation-integration": it entails the right for states to take preventive measures even in the absence of rules providing for that and it entails for them the right to demand from others the prevention of transborder and global risks.[72] In the arbitral award regarding the *Iron Rhine Railway*, for example, the tribunal considered that the principle of integration of environmental protection considerations into all development actions is firmly established in international law;[73] this approach can be transposed beyond the transboundary context to cover global risks.

66 G. de Lassus Saint-Geniès, "Climat", at 192, in M. Cornu, F. Orsi, J. Rochfeld (eds), *Dictionnaire des biens communs*, Paris, PUF, 2017, XXVIII–1240 p. and F. Soltau, "Common concern of Humankind", at 202, in K.R. Gray, R. Tarasofsky, C. Carlarne (eds), *The Oxford handbook of international climate change law*, OUP, 2016, XXIV–822 p.

67 "[C]limate change is a common concern of mankind", UNGA, *Protection of global climate for present and future generations of mankind*, resolution 43/53, 6 December 1988, § 1.

68 The notion of common concern is used in treaties of several fields, notably in the International Convention for the regulation of Whaling of 1946, in the Antarctic Treaty, in the Convention to combat Desertification, in the Convention on Biological Diversity …

69 "2. In order to ensure the exercise of the right to health, the States Parties agree to recognise health as a public good".

70 S. Negri, *Salute pubblica, sicurezza e diritti umani nel diritto internazionale, op. cit.*, at 45 et seq.

71 See *infra*, Chapter 4, 2.2.

72 M.M. Mbengue, *Essai sur une théorie du risque en droit international public. L'anticipation du risque environnemental et sanitaire, op. cit.*, at 15.

73 PCA, *Iron Rhine Arbitration (Belgium/Netherlands)*, Award, 24 May 2005, § 59.

3.2 *Mainstreaming Global Risks at the International Level*

The first consequence of the integration principle is the process of "mainstreaming" between international legal regimes. Martti Koskenniemi considers that each regime tends to have a hegemonic posture by considering its own interests as universal and as overriding. Mainstreaming is a mechanism of regime interaction that allows elements of a legal regime to integrate with another in order to become a shared concern.[74] The integration principle indicates which concerns should be mainstreamed, but international law offers states several tools for achieving this objective. A first method, when possible, is systemic integration according to the law of treaties. Article 31, § 3, c) of the Vienna Convention on the Law of Treaties states that, when interpreting a treaty "3. There shall be taken into account, together with the context: ... (c) any relevant rules of international law applicable in the relations between the parties". International courts and tribunals in particular tend to use this possibility to integrate global risks pertaining to climate change and pandemics into the legal regimes they are meant to implement. The *Institut de droit international* in 2021 adopted a resolution on epidemics and pandemics aimed precisely at underlining the necessity to integrate rules of various origins through systemic interpretation: "1. The rules of international law relating to epidemics and other relevant rules of international law should, to the extent possible, be identified, interpreted, applied and implemented as coherent obligations, in line with the principles of harmonisation and systemic integration, in order to avoid conflicts between obligations, as well as the due diligence obligation and the need for international solidarity and cooperation in responding the threats of epidemics. 'Other relevant rules' include inter alia rules of international environmental law, international trade and investment law, international intellectual property law, international transport law, international law on peace and security and international humanitarian law ...".[75]

International courts and tribunals often follow this method when they have to interpret safeguard or exception clauses. "The 'systemic integration' principle of the customary rules of treaty interpretation requires judicial 'interpretive reintegration' of formally separate legal regimes".[76] That is precisely the

74 M. Koskenniemi, "Hegemonic regimes", at 305, in M.A. Young, *Regime interaction in international law*, Cambridge University Press, 2012, x–334 p.

75 *Institut de droit international*, Resolution on Epidemics, Pandemics and International Law of 4 September 2021, Article 7 – Interrelationship among Relevant Rules.

76 E.U. Petersmann, *Multilevel constitutionalism for multilevel governance of public goods: methodology problems in international law, op. cit.*, at 123. See also ILC, *Conclusions of the Study Group on the fragmentation of international law: difficulties arising from the diversification and expansion of international law*, §§ 410 and 488.

purpose of the 1994 WTO Decision on Trade and Environment.[77] Sometimes mainstreaming is achieved between regimes that are not conflictual but simply ignore each other. This was the case with climate law and the regime of protection of the atmosphere (mainly of the ozone layer). The Montreal Protocol was adapted by the Kigali Amendment in 2016 to harmonise its approach with that of the climate change regime: hydrofluorocarbons are now regulated by both legal regimes. The protocol introduces a climate protection objective into the regime concerning the protection of the ozone layer – which is rather efficient – thus creating a convergence between the two regimes.[78] In several other cases, regimes which, for example, regulate activities producing many GHG emissions clearly conflict with norms related to the fight against global risks. They can also be amended to take these external concerns into account. We can mention the cases of the recent adoption within the International Civil Aviation Organisation (ICAO) of the carbon offsetting and reduction scheme for international aviation (CORSIA), which entered into force in 2019 and which created a carbon market to limit the sector's GHG emissions while explicitly referring to the UNFCCC and the Paris Agreement. In a similar fashion, the IMO Initial Strategy on the reduction of GHG emissions from shipping has led to amendments to the International Convention for the Prevention of Pollution from Ships (MARPOL), also with a direct reference to the Paris Agreement.

Concerns about the protection of the environment and health generally, and more precisely about protection against global risks threatening them, have also started to be integrated into several regimes in the ambit of international economic law.[79] Foreign investment law, for example, provides several methods for achieving this aim. Economic treaties can expressly recognise the power of states to take measures to preserve these interests, as is the case with Article 8.9 of the CETA.[80] Investment treaties can also include not lowering standards clauses in order to prevent the state from reneging on

77 1994 Ministerial Decision on Trade and Environment, <https://www.wto.org/english/docs_e/legal_e/56-dtenv.pdf>.

78 See on this issue P. Minnerop, "Climate Protection Agreements", *MPEPIL*, 2018.

79 On this issue see, among others, P.-M. Dupuy, J.E. Viñuales (eds), *Harnessing foreign investment to promote environmental protection. Incentives and safeguards*, Cambridge University Press, 2013, XXVIII–470 p.; P. Acconci, "The integration of non-investment concerns as an opportunity for the modernisation of international investment law: is a multilateral approach desirable?", in G. Sacerdoti, P. Acconci, M. Valenti, A.P. De Luca (eds), *General interests of host states in international investment law*, Cambridge University Press, 2014, XVI–462 p.

80 "For the purpose of this Chapter, the Parties reaffirm their right to regulate within their territories to achieve legitimate policy objectives, such as the protection of public health, safety, the environment [...]".

its international commitments relating to the fight against global risks by way of promoting foreign investments; Article 17 of the 2017 BIT between Japan and Israel states, for instance, "[e]ach Contracting Party recognises that it is inappropriate to encourage investment activities of investors of the other Contracting Party and of a non-Contracting Party by relaxing its domestic health, safety, environmental and labor standards legislation". States can insert into their economic agreements inclusive references to the fight against global risks as a common objective, which is the case with Article 12.6, § 3,[81] of the EU-Singapore Free-Trade Agreement in relation to climate change. Finally, new agreements can be concluded in order effectively to mainstream concerns over global risks. This is the case with the current negotiation by several members of the WTO of the Environmental Goods Agreement, which aims to eliminate tariffs on products that are useful for achieving climate protection goals. The current working draft of a WHO convention, agreement or other international instrument on pandemic prevention, preparedness and response (the "WHO CA+") of 13 July 2022[82] is almost entirely devoted to the integration and coordination of different international legal regimes in order to address the challenge of preventing the global risk of pandemics. The preamble first recognises "that the international spread of disease is a global threat with serious consequences for public health, human lives and economies that calls for the widest possible international cooperation and the participation of all countries in an effective, appropriate and comprehensive international response" and reaffirms "the importance of a One Health approach and the necessity of synergies between multisectoral collaboration at the national and international levels to safeguard human health, detect and prevent health threats at the interface of animal and human ecosystems". Article 2 should concern specifically the relationship with international agreements and instruments by providing that the Parties commit to interpreting existing agreements so as to be synergistic with the WHO CA+ and to concluding further agreements by ensuring that they are compatible with it and, in this perspective, they are to communicate these new agreements to the governance bodies of WHO CA+. If this draft finally leads to

81 "3. The Parties affirm their commitment to reaching the ultimate objective of the UN Framework Convention on Climate Change (hereinafter referred to as 'UNFCCC'), and to effectively implementing the UNFCCC, its Kyoto Protocol, and the Paris Agreement of 12 December 2015 in a manner consistent with the principles and provisions of the UNFCCC. They commit to work together to strengthen the multilateral, rules-based regime under the UNFCCC building on the UNFCCC's agreed decisions, and to support efforts to develop a post-2020 international climate change agreement under the UNFCCC applicable to all parties".

82 A/INB/2/3.

the conclusion of a convention, it could represent a turn towards an integrative approach to global risks at the international level.

From another point of view, the draft's preamble refers to the fact that "pandemic prevention, preparedness and response must be systemically integrated into whole-of-government and whole-of-society approaches", this statement constituting another part of the answer to the global nature of the pandemic risk. The need to bring all the stakeholders together in order to fight pandemics can be answered following the example of existing public-private partnerships (PPP) in the health sector. Some of these PPPs, which include states, international organisations, companies, NGOs, research institutes and philanthropic foundations, have made medicines accessible in the most disadvantaged states. The UN Secretary General has defined them as "voluntary and collaborative relationships between various parties, both state and non-state, in which all participants agree to work together to achieve a common purpose or undertake a specific task and to share risks and responsibilities, resources and benefits".[83] Keeping in mind that they have different forms and structures,[84] among these PPPs are Roll back malaria partnership, Stop TB partnership, GAVI, the Global fund to fight AIDS, tuberculosis and malaria etc.

The cooperation through PPPs is also being tried out to tackle climate change, but mostly at the domestic level, some international institutions providing guidelines to the different interested actors in order to develop these tools.[85] But some of these partnerships have also been created at the international level, mainly on a regional scale. One of them is the Pacific Resilience Partnership, established by the Pacific Island Forum to support the implementation of the Framework for Resilient Development in the Pacific: An Integrated Approach to Address Climate Change and Disaster Risk Management 2017–2030 (FRDP). It brings together the private sector, national and sub-national authorities and regional organisations. Integration of global risks at the international level must be complemented by several means pursuing the same aim in the domestic sphere.

83 UNSG, *Enhanced cooperation between the United Nations and all relevant partners, in particular the private sector*, Report of 10 August 2005, A/60/214, § 8.

84 See, among others, L. Clarke, *Public-private partnerships and responsibility under international law: a global health perspective*, New York, Routledge, 2014, XVIII–252 p.

85 See for instance <https://ppp.worldbank.org/public-private-partnership/climate-smart-ppps-further-reading-and-resources>.

3.3 *Mainstreaming Global Risks at the Domestic Level*

Integrating global risks at the domestic level means that states should take them into account when elaborating their different public policies. This process must be distinguished from the adoption of national legislation in order to implement international obligations in the fight against those risks. Some domestic courts have highlighted the necessity for states to take these measures in order to fulfil their due diligence obligations. That is the case, for instance, with the Supreme Court of Nepal, which stressed that the state should have implemented its international obligations by enacting a law dealing with climate change.[86] The High Court of New Zealand also decided that the Minister for Climate Change Issues should have reviewed the national target after the issue of the IPCC's Fifth Assessment Report (AR5).[87]

The principle of integration, by contrast, requires wider action consisting of the taking into account of the effects of public policies in relation to global risks within all decision-making processes; it is included with this meaning in several international treaties. The main tool which is required here is the realisation of impact assessments. According to article 4, § 1, f) of the UNFCCC, "1. All Parties, taking into account their common but differentiated responsibilities and their specific national and regional development priorities, objectives and circumstances, shall: … (f) Take climate change considerations into account, to the extent feasible, in their relevant social, economic and environmental policies and actions". This formulation is particularly wide and seems also to encompass strategic impact assessments which are implemented very early, at the planning stage. Several states have introduced this kind of environmental impact assessment into their national legislation.[88] These include South Africa which created a specific "climate change impact assessment" requirement at the ministerial level for many kinds of projects.[89] By analogy, it is interesting to consider the scope of international obligations and other types of international norms on transboundary environmental impact assessments which could shed some light on the way domestic impact assessments should be implemented. The ILC's *Guidelines on the protection of the atmosphere* include

---

86 Supreme Court of Nepal, *Shrestha v. Office of the Prime Minister et al.*, 25 December 2018, at 5.

87 High Court of New Zealand, *Thomson v. Minister for Climate Change Issues*, 2 November 2017, § 94.

88 See A. Van Duyn, "Transboundary environmental impact assessments and the international control of infectious disease spread", at 451–452, in S. Murase, S. Zhou (eds), *Epidemics and international law*, Leiden, Brill Nijhoff, 2021, XXXII–708 p.

89 This issue was at the core of the decision in South Africa's High Court, *EarthLife Africa Johannesburg v. Minister of Environmental Affairs and Others*, 6 March 2017.

among the dangers of atmospheric pollution damage to human health.[90] In a similar way, the Convention on Environmental Impact Assessment in a Transboundary Context (the Espoo Convention) includes among adverse impacts the effects caused "on the environment including human health".[91] Moreover, the Protocol on Strategic Environmental Assessment (Kiev Protocol) of 2003 widens this approach by requiring impact assessments (including with regard to health) in the development of all plans and programmes beyond specific projects (Article 1 (a)), and it is not limited to transboundary effects.[92] The United Nations Economic Commission for Europe's Resource Manual to Support Application of the Protocol considers that this requirement covers "health impact assessments".[93] These procedures have been developed domestically by a number of states[94] and could also include considerations on the necessity for the prevention of epidemics. On the other hand, "[w]hen considering whether to authorise conduct, states should consider infectious disease spread as a component of environmental harm".[95]

Impact assessment tools are also used to integrate human rights concerns into state policies, which is, for example, the case in respect of the right to health. The analysis of a budget through a human rights implementation framework requires the development of specific tools.[96] The Human Rights Council

---

90 "Guideline 1 – Use of terms
For the purposes of the present draft guidelines:
(a) 'atmosphere' means the envelope of gases surrounding the Earth;
(b) 'atmospheric pollution' means the introduction or release by humans, directly or indirectly, into the atmosphere of substances or energy contributing to significant deleterious effects extending beyond the State of origin of such a nature as to endanger human life and health and the Earth's natural environment;
(c) 'atmospheric degradation' means the alteration by humans, directly or indirectly, of atmospheric conditions having significant deleterious effects of such a nature as to endanger human life and health and the Earth's natural environment", *Yearbook of the International Law Commission*, 2021, vol. II, Part 2, at 20.

91 Article 2, § 3.

92 A. Boyle, N. Singh Ghaleigh, "Climate change and international law beyond the UNFCCC", at 26, in K.R. Gray, R. Tarasofsky, C. Carlarne (eds), *The Oxford handbook of international climate change law*, *op. cit.*

93 A. Van Duyn, "Transboundary environmental impact assessments and the international control of infectious disease spread", *op. cit.*, at 457.

94 See the guidelines provided by the WHO: <https://www.who.int/health-topics/health-impact-assessment#tab=tab_1>.

95 A. Van Duyn, "Transboundary environmental impact assessments and the international control of infectious disease spread", *op. cit.*, at 464.

96 On this issue see the substantial proposal of O. De Schutter, "Public budget analysis for the realisation of economic, social and cultural rights: conceptual framework and practical implementation", *op. cit.*

has provided insights into the necessity of implementing human rights impact assessments into economic reforms.[97] These procedures should be carried out before the reform is undertaken and the Council provides recommendations on the specific tools that should be used.[98] Some experts have developed the Social and Economic Rights Fulfilment Index (SERF index) which gave rise to the human rights measurement initiative.[99]

These examples show that strategic impact assessment has already been established in a transboundary context and could thus be transposed to the domestic level; it seems to be particularly well-suited to global risks because it is a means to address a strong indeterminacy on the negative effects of an activity in this context. They also show that environmental and health assessments are experimented on at the domestic level in a number of states and that they are already – and could be in certain cases – extended more specifically to the prevention of climate change and pandemics.

3.4 *Integration between Global Risks*

As we have already noted,[100] the risks of climate change and pandemics intersect in a number of ways. Drawing from this factual basis, the integration of global risks can also be considered through a horizontal point of view, aiming at taking these risks into account at the same time. They are, for example, both included in the One Health approach. The Manhattan Principles on "One World, One Health" build upon the principle of integration of the protection of human health, animal health and the environment in an ecosystemic approach.[101] They first recognise the relationship between the decisions taken in one field over the other interests (Principle 2), and they advocate for the adoption of holistic preventative approaches (Principle 5) and for the fostering of the integration of an environmental perspective with a health perspective (Principle 6).[102]

---

97 Resolution 40/8, *The effects of foreign debt and other related international financial obligations of States on the enjoyment of human rights*, 5 April 2019.

98 Scotland has integrated them for example into the National Performance Framework: <https://nationalperformance.gov.scot/sustainable-development-goals>.

99 A. Corkery, I. Saiz, "Progressive realisation using maximum available resources: the accountability challenge", at 275, in J. Dugard, B. Porter, D. Ikawa, L. Chenwi (eds), *Research handbook on economic, social and cultural rights as human rights*, Cheltenham, Edward Elgar Publishing, 2020, XXVIII–422 p.

100 Cf *supra*, Chapter 1, 4.

101 S. Negri, *Salute pubblica, sicurezza e diritti umani nel diritto internazionale*, *op. cit.*, at 22.

102 J. Zinsstag, E. Schelling, D. Waltner-Toews, M. Whittaker, M. Tanner (eds), *One Health. The Theory and Practice of Integrated Health Approaches*, Wallingford, CABI, XXII–448 p.

This approach is supported by the rationale of the Sustainable Development Goals of the United Nations as adopted by resolution A/RES/70/1 of 21 October 2015 of the General Assembly. The 17 Goals and 169 targets aim at delineating a World Agenda by 2030. The preamble immediately stresses that SDGs are considered to be "integrated and indivisible", an expression which is reiterated several times.[103] The goal related to climate change specifically recognises that "[t]he challenges and commitments ... are interrelated and call for integrated solutions" (§ 13). Even if they are largely programmatic, the SDGs can be used as guidelines in terms of interpretation. When they refer to international conventions, for instance, they can be used to coordinate them, and they can more generally serve to interpret the concept of sustainable development. They can be seen as constituting a first materialisation of global public goods: this seems to be the case in the way the end of an epidemic (Goal 3.3) or the fight against climate change (Goal 13) is formulated.[104] Moreover, the UN has set up indicators[105] to control the implementation of the SDGs and these indicators also have a normative dimension by aiming at modifying the practice of states. Joel Trachtman analyses this integration as a response to "interfunctional linkage": when specific issues are strongly interconnected – which is the case with global risks – action related to one of them necessarily has an impact on the others. He details the various methods that can be used in order to take these links into account, stemming from an economic analysis. Functional integration could thus take the form of the harmonisation of different interests by one institution, or of the creation of a specific institution devoted to several objectives or of the taking into account of external interests by some institutions.[106] The Director General of the WHO drafted in 2019 a report on *WHO global strategy on health, environment and climate change: the transformation needed to improve lives and well-being sustainably through healthy environments.*[107] The proposal builds on the integration principle by suggesting cross-sectoral action

103 See, for instance, "The Sustainable Development Goals and targets are integrated and indivisible, global in nature and universally applicable" (§ 55).

104 W. Huck, "The UN sustainable development goals and the governance of global public goods", at 348, in M. Iovane, F.M. Palombino, D. Amoroso, G. Zarra (eds), *The protection of general interests in contemporary international law*, Oxford University Press, 2021, XX–416 p.

105 UNGA, Resolution 71/313 of 6 July 2017.

106 J. Trachtman, *The economic structure of international law*, Cambridge, Harvard University Press, 2008, at 205.

107 Health, environment and climate change - Draft WHO global strategy on health, environment and climate change: the transformation needed to improve lives and well-being sustainably through healthy environments, A72/15, 18 April 2019.

taking into account both environmental and health risks, for example in the sectors of energy and transport.

Another point of view consists in considering that the most efficient harmonisation could be realised at the domestic level, and thus that states should try to balance the considerations of different global risks. This position has been supported by the UN Committee on Social, Economic and Cultural Rights, which issued in 2018 a statement on the methods states should use when defining their NDCs of the Paris Agreement in order to take into account social rights such as the right to health. Their human rights obligations are meant to guide them in the implementation of measures aimed at fighting climate change. From this standpoint, "a failure to prevent foreseeable human rights harm caused by climate change, or a failure to mobilise the maximum available resources in an effort to do so, could constitute a breach" of these obligations.[108] The integration approach, while probably not having already attained the status of a legal principle of international law, is reflected in several international hard and soft law norms and produces several effects at the international level as well as at the national level. It will probably develop in the next few years because it is crucial for tackling global risks such as climate change and pandemics.

One specific means of integration is the due diligence standard that characterises most state obligations in the field of global risks.

4 The Central Function of Due Diligence Standards

Black's Law Dictionary defines due diligence as "the diligence reasonably expected from, and ordinarily exercised by, a person who seeks to satisfy a legal requirement or to discharge an obligation".[109] In all legal fields it is a qualification attached to a duty of care, a way of carrying out some kind of obligation. In international law due diligence finds its origins in the no harm rule which requires states to ensure that no harm is caused to another state from their territory or from a situation over which they exercise effective control.[110] Its

108 Climate change and the International Covenant on Economic, Social and Cultural Rights, Statement of the Committee on Economic, Social and Cultural Rights, 8 October 2018, <https://www.ohchr.org/en/statements/2018/10/committee-releases-statement-climate-change-and-covenant>.

109 B.A. Garner, "Due diligence", at 553, in *Black's Law Dictionary*, St. Paul (MN): West Publishing, 10th ed., 2014.

110 See the *Trail smelter case* (*United States, Canada*), 16 April 1938 and 11 March 1941, *UN Reports of International Arbitral Awards*, vol. III, at 1905–1982. See also, "[t]he existence

scope, first limited to activities under the territorial jurisdiction of states, has thus been much extended in the context of global risks. Due diligence standards are a means of placing the responsibility for the fight against global risks mainly on states, which are thus supposed to control the activity of other actors – above all private actors – under their jurisdiction. This is an example of how due diligence works both as a response to and a catalyst for structural changes in international law.[111] Combined with the notion of "common concern of humankind", which is applicable to global public goods such as the climate and health, due diligence standards contribute to the development of state obligations and responsibility.[112] In this sense, due diligence is a means of overcoming the difficulties of capturing complex risks such as climate change and pandemics because it extends beyond a transboundary framework.[113]

More precisely, due diligence qualifies obligations of prevention and precaution which are rather frequent in the fight against global risks (4.1). The implementation of these due diligence obligations requires the identification of specific standards in order to evaluate the diligence – or negligence – of the state in a specific case. These standards are put into effect through the interaction of different types of international norms (4.2) and through the complementarity of international and national law (4.3) in the fight against global risks.

4.1 *Due Diligence Obligations in the Context of Global Risks*

Due diligence obligations are strongly linked to the emergence of global risks and to the necessity of avoiding what Ulrich Beck refers to as "organised irresponsibility".[114] "Even where activities are not meant to cross borders, they may spill over state frontiers not least in relation to global commons".[115]

---

of the general obligation of States to ensure that activities within their jurisdiction and control respect the environment of other States or of areas beyond national control is now part of the corpus of international law relating to the environment", ICJ, *Legality of the Threat or Use of Nuclear Weapons*, *op. cit.*, § 29.

111 H. Krieger, A. Peters, "Due diligence and structural change in the international legal order", at 351, in H. Krieger, A. Peters, L. Kreuzer (eds), *Due diligence in the international legal order*, Oxford University Press, 2020, XVIII–402 p.

112 See on this issue the point of view of V. Vadi, "Beyond known worlds: climate change governance by arbitral tribunals?", *Vanderbilt Journal of transnational Law*, 2015, at 1329.

113 S. Besson, "La *due diligence* en droit international", *Collected Courses of The Hague Academy of International Law*, 2020, vol. 409, at 201–202.

114 U. Beck, *op. cit.*, at 58–59.

115 H. Krieger, A. Peters, « Due diligence and structural change in the international legal order", at 353, in H. Krieger, A. Peters, L. Kreuzer (eds), *Due diligence in the international legal order*, Oxford University Press, 2020, XVIII–402 p.

This is manifest first in relation to the global risk of climate change. International obligations of states in this area meet a standard of due diligence, which refers to both multiple obligations of means and obligations of result. The general obligation to prevent risks arising from climate change can only be an obligation of means: the final result also depends on the behaviour of all other states and many other actors which constitutes a significant hazard. But this general obligation also includes a number of more specific obligations, including to carry out environmental impact assessments when a major project is planned, which is, for example, an obligation of result. In addition, the customary obligation not to cause harm to other states from one's own territory is also an obligation of means. In the UNFCCC examples of due diligence obligations include those mentioned in Article 4, which require best efforts on the part of the state.[116] The turn to procedural obligations of the Paris Agreement also leaves much room for due diligence, mainly in relation to mitigation obligations. In this sense, Article 4 § 2 contains an example of a due diligence obligation with an implicit reference to the best efforts of states parties.[117]

The first constitutive element of due diligence is the state's knowledge of the existence of the climate risk; this is currently easily proved through the IPCC's periodical reports, which provide the best scientific updated knowledge on climate change and its detrimental effects. The second element is the link that must exist between the state and the activity causing the damage it ought to be preventing, which could be called the "risk proximity".[118] The no-harm rule was first based on territoriality, but its scope has evolved since the beginning of the 20th Century. Climate rules clearly include a larger conception of this link: according to the preamble to the UNFCCC, "[s]tates have, in accordance with the Charter of the United Nations and the principles of international law, … the responsibility to ensure that activities within their

116 See for instance § 1 f): « (f) Take climate change considerations into account, to the extent feasible, in their relevant social, economic and environmental policies and actions, and employ appropriate methods, for example impact assessments, formulated and determined nationally, with a view to minimising adverse effects on the economy, on public health and on the quality of the environment, of projects or measures undertaken by them to mitigate or adapt to climate change ».

117 « 2. Each Party shall prepare, communicate and maintain successive nationally determined contributions that it intends to achieve. Parties shall pursue domestic mitigation measures, with the aim of achieving the objectives of such contributions ». See the table presenting a classification of the Paris Agreement obligations proposed by D. Bodansky, J. Brunnée, L. Rajamani, *International climate change law*, *op. cit.*, at 213 *et seq.*

118 This expression is used by F. Violi, "The function of the triad 'territory', 'jurisdiction', and 'control' in due diligence obligations", at 75, in H. Krieger, A. Peters, L. Kreuzer (eds), *Due diligence in the international legal order*, Oxford University Press, 2020, XVIII–402 p.

jurisdiction or control do not cause damage to the environment of other States or of areas beyond the limits of national jurisdiction". It thus includes activities under both the *jurisdiction* and the *control* of states parties. In relation to adaptation, article 7, § 2, of the Paris Agreement follows the same rationale: "[p]arties recognise that adaptation is a global challenge faced by all with local, subnational, national, regional and international dimensions, and that it is a key component of and makes a contribution to the long-term global response to climate change to protect people, livelihoods and ecosystems, taking into account the urgent and immediate needs of those developing country Parties that are particularly vulnerable to the adverse effects of climate change". Taking complementary obligations stemming from other international legal regimes into account, Article 194 of UNCLOS uses the same criteria for the obligation to prevent damage to the marine environment.[119] The Inter-American

119 "Measures to prevent, reduce and control pollution of the marine environment

1. States shall take, individually or jointly as appropriate, all measures consistent with this Convention that are necessary to prevent, reduce and control pollution of the marine environment from any source, using for this purpose the best practicable means at their disposal and in accordance with their capabilities, and they shall endeavour to harmonise their policies in this connection.
2. States shall take all measures necessary to ensure that activities under their jurisdiction or control are so conducted as not to cause damage by pollution to other States and their environment, and that pollution arising from incidents or activities under their jurisdiction or control does not spread beyond the areas where they exercise sovereign rights in accordance with this Convention.
3. The measures taken pursuant to this Part shall deal with all sources of pollution of the marine environment. These measures shall include, inter alia, those designed to minimise to the fullest possible extent:
   (a) the release of toxic, harmful or noxious substances, especially those which are persistent, from land-based sources, from or through the atmosphere or by dumping;
   (b) pollution from vessels, in particular measures for preventing accidents and dealing with emergencies, ensuring the safety of operations at sea, preventing intentional and unintentional discharges, and regulating the design, construction, equipment, operation and manning of vessels;
   (c) pollution from installations and devices used in exploration or exploitation of the natural resources of the seabed and subsoil, in particular measures for preventing accidents and dealing with emergencies, ensuring the safety of operations at sea, and regulating the design, construction, equipment, operation and manning of such installations or devices;
   (d) pollution from other installations and devices operating in the marine environment, in particular measures for preventing accidents and dealing with emergencies, ensuring the safety of operations at sea, and regulating the design, construction, equipment, operation and manning of such installations or devices.

Court of Human Rights confirmed the extraterritorial scope of the obligations stemming from the right to a healthy environment which are also relevant in the context of climate change.[120]

The last and most important element of the evaluation of the due diligence obligation is the use by the state of all reasonable means at its disposal to prevent the damage. The assessment of this criterion needs in every case to determine a reference standard of due diligence; the elements of this standard in relation to climate obligations can be found in the UNFCCC and the Paris Agreement. The first component of this due diligence standard lies in the objectives and guiding principles laid down, for example, in Article 3 of the UNFCC – which mentions equity, common but differentiated responsibilities, respective capabilities etc. – and in Articles 2 and 3 of the Paris Agreement, which refer to the same principles and to "ambitious efforts", "a progression over time" of the efforts and the leadership of developed states in the implementation of NDCs. The second component is a margin of appreciation left to the parties as provided by Article 4 of the UNFCCC, according to which the parties participate to the response to climate change in accordance with their "respective capabilities and their social and economic conditions". Article 5 of the Paris Agreement also refers to the improvement in sinks and reservoirs of greenhouse gases "as appropriate". A third component is differentiation in the implementation of the obligations according to the level of development of each state, as illustrated by the example of Article 2, § 2, of the Paris Agreement: "This Agreement will be implemented to reflect equity and the principle of common but differentiated responsibilities and respective capabilities, in the light of different national circumstances".[121] These criteria, necessary to give content to general state obligations and to assess their implementation, are complemented by the 2018 Paris Rulebook adopted by the COP 24 in Katowice, which details the procedural obligations contained in the Paris

---

4. In taking measures to prevent, reduce or control pollution of the marine environment, States shall refrain from unjustifiable interference with activities carried out by other States in the exercise of their rights and in pursuance of their duties in conformity with this Convention.
5. The measures taken in accordance with this Part shall include those necessary to protect and preserve rare or fragile ecosystems as well as the habitat of depleted, threatened or endangered species and other forms of marine life".

120 Interamerican Court of Human Rights, *A Request for an Advisory Opinion from the Inter-American Court of Human Rights Concerning the Interpretation of Article 1(1), 4(1) and 5(1) of the American Convention on Human Rights*), 15 November 2017, § 82.

121 On this issue see L. Rajamani, "Due diligence in international climate change law", at 163, in H. Krieger, A. Peters, L. Kreuzer (eds), *Due diligence in the international legal order*, Oxford University Press, 2020, XVIII–402 p.

Agreement, such as the list of information items of its NDC which each Party has to notify to the others; in this way, the content of state obligations is determined by the combination of hard and soft-law norms.

As regards the fight against the global risk of pandemics, states' obligations have different origins. First, a series of obligations to prevent and respond to public health emergencies of international concern in order to anticipate the emergence of epidemics can be found in the WHO's International Health Regulations, to which 196 states are parties. Second, several health obligations arise out of the right to health, as provided for in human rights treaties and as enshrined in decisions of international courts and of quasi-judicial bodies.[122] Third, states must respect the customary no-harm rule, which includes the prevention of damage to the health of populations of other states. While the general obligation to use all available means to prevent the occurrence of a pandemic is a due diligence obligation, because of the high degree of uncertainty that characterises this situation, we can distinguish within this legal framework the different types of obligations that make up and specify it.

Most pandemic prevention obligations are obligations of means, so that an international wrongful act is done if the state has failed to use its best efforts, regardless of the outcome, which depends also on a multitude of other factors. This is the case with Articles 24 and 34 of the International Health Regulations, which oblige states to exercise control over the actions of conveyance operators and container shippers. This is also the case with the obligation of prevention stemming from the customary no-harm rule, as recognised by the International Court of Justice.[123] Among the obligations of means, several have the particularity of being formulated in a largely indeterminate manner, leaving

122 Article 12 of the International Covenant on Economic, Social and Cultural Rights provides the broadest definition of the right to health. Several sectoral conventions at the universal level also include it. These include Article 24(1) of the International Convention on the Rights of the Child or Article 5 of the International Convention on the Elimination of All Forms of Racial Discrimination. At the regional level, it is included in Article 16 of the African Charter on Human and Peoples' Rights, in Article 11 of the European Social Charter and in Article 10 of the Additional Protocol to the American Convention on Human Rights in the Area of Economic, Social and Cultural Rights. Although the European Convention on Human Rights does not mention the right to health, the European Court of Human Rights has enshrined several positive obligations relating to the protection of health, pursuant to Articles 2 (right to life), 3 (prohibition of torture) and 8 (right to respect for private and family life).

123 "A State is thus obliged to use all the means at its disposal in order to avoid activities which take place in its territory, or in any area under its jurisdiction, causing significant damage to the environment of another State", ICJ, *Pulp Mills on the River Uruguay* (*Argentina v. Uruguay*), Judgment, 20 April 2010, § 101.

a significant margin of appreciation to states for their implementation. As they are to be implemented over the long term, they appear to be non-autonomous "multi-tiered obligations" that refer to a series of more specific obligations the application of which can be assessed on a case-by-case basis. This assessment largely corresponds to that of obligations of means, but the progressive realisation of these obligations is highly dependent on the context characterising each phase of their application. The right to health, for example, is broadly progressive, but it involves many obligations to take ongoing measures the implementation of which can be assessed at any given point in time. This type of obligation is also found in Article 44 of the International Health Regulations concerning technical and logistical cooperation between states in the implementation of their health obligations. Articles 5 (surveillance and monitoring capacity) and 13 (capacity to respond to public health risks) also contain obligations that require a sustained effort. While all these obligations meet the standard of due diligence, their implementation poses varying challenges.

The evidence of a state's negligence relates here too to its knowledge of the existence of a global epidemic risk. With regard to the implementation of obligations to prevent the spread of an epidemic such as COVID-19, this knowledge is established at least following the declaration of this type of health emergency by the Director General of the WHO. The implementation of certain progressive obligations is more complex, as one goes back in time in order to determine at what moment the state acted neglectfully in the face of its knowledge of the risk. For example, can it be considered that France had sufficient knowledge of the global risk of a pandemic when, in 2013, it decided not to renew its strategic stockpile of masks, to result in a violation of Article 13 of the IHR and of the right to health of the people present on its territory at the outbreak of the COVID-19 pandemic?[124]

The second evaluation criterion concerns the control exercised by the state over the risk of epidemic. Each state is at least deemed to have control over the risk of the spread of an epidemic on its territory in terms of its various prevention obligations. However, it can be considered that states also exercise control over private actors, including companies, whose actions have an impact on this overall risk. Article 24 of the International Health Regulations, for example, requires states to exercise control over operators of means of transport who are directly involved in preventing the spread of the epidemic. Similarly, the right to health implies an obligation on states to provide access to essential medicines, but its implementation may conflict with the intellectual property

124 A. Coco, T. De Souza, "Due Diligence and COVID-19: States' Duties to Prevent and Halt the Coronavirus Outbreak", *EJIL Talk!*, 24 March 2020.

rights of pharmaceutical companies, as was evident in the case of access to vaccines against COVID-19. While the Declaration on the TRIPS Agreement and Public Health adopted by the WTO on 14 November 2001 allows for waivers in situations of health emergencies, so-called "TRIPS-plus" clauses in various trade agreements nullify their effects, in violation of the right to health. In these cases, state control of private actors (both natural and legal persons) may depend on the criteria of nationality or of the application of domestic law to companies.

Finally, the content of the wrongful negligence consists in the failure to use reasonable means to deal with the risk. The standard of due diligence requires consideration of the means available to each state, and therefore the same degree of requirement for health response capabilities cannot be demanded of all states, depending in particular on their level of development. Moreover, the global nature of pandemics means that measures to address them are likely to have adverse effects on other interests that are also subject to international obligations. Containment measures, for example, affect not only economic interests but also a wide range of fundamental rights. Taking these interests into account in determining the appropriate health measures for the different phases of the pandemic may therefore seem reasonable. A complementary approach to assessing the reasonableness of the means employed by states relies on soft-law instruments that allow the content of the various obligations to be concretised. For example, the WHO has developed a series of indicators for this purpose. Similarly, in the event of a health emergency of international concern, the International Health Regulations allow the Director-General to issue temporary recommendations to states with a view to their adapting their health measures to each phase of the situation. The ILC's 2016 Draft Articles on the Protection of Persons in the Event of Disasters may also provide guidance on the interpretation of states' obligations,[125] and several UN agencies and non-governmental actors have developed indicators to assess the level of implementation of the right to health.[126]

---

125 This instrument includes obligations to reduce the risk (Art. 9), to ensure the protection of persons in the event of disasters (Art. 10 and 16), to seek assistance when the situation exceeds the state's capacity (Art. 11), to take all measures to bring in external assistance (Art. 15).

126 See, e.g., OHCHR, *Human rights indicators – A guide to measurement and implementation*, HR/PUB/12/5 (30 March 2012) and on this issue A.E. Yamin, "The right to health", at 159–179, in J. Dugard, B. Porter, D. Ikawa, L. Chenwi (eds), *Research handbook on economic, social and cultural rights as human rights*, Cheltenham, Edward Elgar Publishing, 2020, XXVIII–422 p.

While meeting the same criteria, the assessment of the reasonableness of measures adopted under obligations that are to be implemented over the long term depends on exact timing. Under the International Health Regulations, for example, the deadline for implementation of the obligations of Articles 5 and 13 was 2016, with Annex 1 providing criteria for this. But when considering the obligation to establish a health system capable of responding to emergencies, only total inaction is easy to assess. For the many obligations contained therein it is necessary to take careful account of the circumstances at a given moment. Several decisions on stockpiling health supplies, for example, are adopted by states long before epidemics occur. The Committee on Economic, Social and Cultural Rights has indicated that the allocation of an insufficient budget to establish a rapid response system for health emergencies may constitute a violation of state obligations under the right to health.[127] However, compliance with the obligation in this case must be assessed *ex tunc* and raises serious questions of causality.[128] In this way, due diligence gives effect to health obligations of progressive realisation or "goal-oriented" obligations[129].

For both global risks, in order to avoid the free rider problem by fostering cooperation, the transmission of information – and thus transparency – on the behaviour and situation of each state, and thus on the costs and benefits of different options of action, is needed.[130] Several due diligence procedural obligations are useful in this respect, such as the duty to give notice of activities that may cause significant harm to other states or to common areas; the duty to provide access to relevant information with which to address the risk from the activity; and the duty to consult about the activity.

In conclusion, it is possible to say that due diligence now applies beyond the interests of states to the interest of environmental and public health protection *per se*, thus requiring extraterritorial application and potentially application even when the harm threatens the state's own territory.[131]

127 CESCR, General Comment No 14 (2000), *op. cit.*, § 52.

128 L. Bottini Filho, "State positive obligations and the international right to health in epidemics: how much should be enough?", at 389, in S. Murase, S. Zhou (eds), *Epidemics and international law*, Leiden, Brill Nijhoff, 2021, XXXII–708 p.

129 H. Krieger, A. Peters, "Due diligence and structural change in the international legal order", at 351, in H. Krieger, A. Peters, L. Kreuzer (eds), *Due diligence in the international legal order*, Oxford University Press, 2020, XVIII–402 p.

130 E. Brown Weiss, *op. cit.*, at 124.

131 See, concerning the environment, J.E. Viñuales, "Due diligence in international environmental law", at 111, in H. Krieger, A. Peters, L. Kreuzer (eds), *Due diligence in the international legal order*, Oxford University Press, 2020, XVIII–402 p.

4.2 *Determination of due Diligence Standards through the Interaction of International Legal Regimes*

From the point of view of primary rules, due diligence allows the development of law in under-regulated areas by giving content to vague positive obligations, which is possible mainly through regime interaction.[132] The concretisation of each due diligence standard allows specific provisions of a treaty to be linked to external legal regimes; according to some authors, it is a factor favourable to the inclusion of open-ended clauses in treaties while leaving to treaty implementation the task of articulating conflicting interests in each case.[133] The International Tribunal for the Law of the Sea (ITLOS) stated in an advisory opinion that some "direct" state obligations deriving from the UNCLOS are not due diligence obligations, but that their implementation may be considered a pertinent factor in assessing compliance with the general due diligence "obligation to ensure".[134]

A court faced with the invocation of state liability for environmental damage related to sea level rise or to damage caused by climate change to the marine environment, for example, is forced into a reconstruction exercise aimed at determining what measures a diligent state should have adopted. The combination of climate change law and the law of the sea tends, however, to make it easier to concretise this diligence standard. The determination of the content of these reasonable measures is facilitated by the articulation between climate law and the law of the sea regimes through due diligence. The latter is presented as a specific area in which climate obligations of states apply, and, conversely, the provisions of UNCLOS can be read in the light of those of the Paris Agreement. Articles 194 and 207 of UNCLOS refer to rules and standards from other areas of international law and thus potentially to the Paris Agreement in the context of marine environmental protection. According to the latter treaty, the mitigation obligations it provides for are

132 A. Peters, H. Krieger, L. Kreuzer, "Due diligence in the international legal order. Dissecting the leitmotiv of current accountability debates", at 1, in H. Krieger, A. Peters, L. Kreuzer (eds), *Due diligence in the international legal order*, Oxford University Press, 2020, XVIII–402 p.

133 H. Krieger, A. Peters, "Due diligence and structural change in the international legal order", at 351, in H. Krieger, A. Peters, L. Kreuzer (eds), *Due diligence in the international legal order*, Oxford University Press, 2020, XVIII–402 p.

134 ITLOS, *Responsibilities and obligations of States sponsoring persons and entities with respect to activities in the Area* (*Request for Advisory Opinion submitted to the Seabed Disputes Chamber*), advisory opinion, 1 February 2011, §§ 121–123. See also S. Forlati, "L'objet des différentes obligations primaires de diligence: prévention, cessation, répression ... ?", in SFDI, *Le standard de due diligence et la responsabilité internationale. Journée d'études franco-italienne du Mans*, Paris, Pedone, 2018, at 46.

evolutionary and the means constituted by NDCs produce a ratchet effect (Article 3), while remaining within the framework of the general objective as defined by the Agreement. Article 4 of the Paris Agreement also refers to an evolving due diligence obligation to be implemented "as soon as possible" and with the "highest possible level of ambition". It can be inferred that "in the context of LOSC Part XII the Paris Agreement sets out the 'necessary measures' and 'generally accepted international rules and standards' for protecting and preserving the marine environment from the deleterious effects of GHG emissions and climate change, whether through acidification or warming of seawater, or sea-level rise".[135] Moreover, while the ITLOS has clearly stated that the application of due diligence obligations under UNCLOS is not subject to a differentiation regime,[136] the articulation with the climate law regime in the assessment of obligations to protect the marine environment allows for the consideration of common but differentiated responsibilities and respective capabilities, as referred to in the Paris Agreement. In the light of these guidelines, a whole series of specific obligations – of means as well as of result – in the law of the sea which specify the reasonable means of implementing the general obligation of diligence can be identified and concretised.[137] These include the adoption of rules and administrative acts, vigilance in the application of those acts, the adoption of enforcement measures including at the judicial level, the creation of monitoring mechanisms, the use of precautionary measures and the implementation of environmental impact assessments.[138] The complementarity between climate law and the law of the sea should provide a fairly precise frame of reference regarding the reasonable means to be used.

In relation to states' obligations to prevent epidemics, some authors consider that a specific due diligence standard can be derived from the articulation of obligations of the IHR with obligations stemming from the right to health and climate obligations contained in the Paris Agreement.[139] This

135 A. Boyle, "Protecting the marine environment from climate change. The LOSC Part XII regime", at 102, in E. Johansen, S.V. Busch, I.U. Jakobsen (eds), *The law of the sea and climate change. Solutions and constraints*, Cambridge University Press, 2021, XXVI–436 p.

136 ITLOS, *Responsibilities and obligations of States sponsoring persons and entities with respect to activities in the Area (Request for Advisory Opinion submitted to the Seabed Disputes Chamber)*, *op. cit.*, § 158.

137 I. Papanicolopulu, "Due diligence in the law of the sea", at 158–159, in H. Krieger, A. Peters, L. Kreuzer (eds), *Due diligence in the international legal order*, Oxford University Press, 2020, XVIII–402 p.

138 ITLOS, *Responsibilities and obligations of States sponsoring persons and entities with respect to activities in the Area (Request for Advisory Opinion submitted to the Seabed Disputes Chamber)*, *op. cit.*, §§ 104–145.

139 I. A. Giménez, "Epidemics and climate change in international law", at 412, in S. Murase, S. Zhou (eds), *Epidemics and international law*, Leiden, Brill Nijhoff, 2021, XXXII–708 p.

obligation of due diligence is also objectified within specific contexts by reference to rules belonging to other legal regimes. Obligations to prevent, reduce and control epidemics are indeed also found in several maritime and civil aviation law agreements, such as in Article 14 of the Chicago Convention on International Civil Aviation on the prevention of spread of disease[140] or in Article 2 of the International Convention on Ballast Control and Management.[141]

The International Court of Justice considers that the obligation of prevention finds its origin in the notion of due diligence and includes conducting an environmental impact assessment as soon as an activity under the control of the state is likely to have an impact beyond its borders.[142] But some due diligence obligations go beyond mere prevention through their interaction with a precautionary approach.[143] The European Court of Human Rights has also based its reasoning on the precautionary principle to develop the scope of the obligations to prevent environmental and health risks included among the positive obligations of Article 8 of the Convention on the protection of private and family life. It thus recognised a violation of the Convention by Romania because of the passivity of the public authorities in respect of the consequences of an industrial accident, when scientific knowledge did not allow the precise identification of the risks at stake.[144] These positive obligations are particularly extensive, in that they also apply to the activities of private actors. A precautionary approach can reinforce due diligence obligations of states such as the assessment of the impact of risky activities taking

140 "Each contracting State agrees to take effective measures to prevent the spread by means of air navigation of cholera, typhus (epidemic), smallpox, yellow fever, plague, and such other communicable diseases as the contracting States shall from time to time decide to designate, and to that end contracting States will keep in close consultation with the agencies concerned with international regulations relating to sanitary measurer, applicable to aircraft. Such consultation shall be without prejudice to the application of any existing international convention on this subject to which the contracting States may be parties".

141 On this issue see S. Murase, "Interrelationship among relevant rules of international law on epidemics", at 19, in S. Murase, S. Zhou (eds), *Epidemics and international law*, Leiden, Brill Nijhoff, 2021, XXXII–708 p.

142 ICJ, *Pulp Mills on the River Uruguay (Argentina v. Uruguay)*, *op. cit.*, § 204 and ICJ, *Certain Activities Carried Out by Nicaragua in the Border Area (Costa Rica v. Nicaragua) and Construction of a Road in Costa Rica along the San Juan River (Nicaragua v. Costa Rica)*, Judgment, 16 December 2015, § 104. See also D. Bodansky, J. Brunnée, L. Rajamani, *International climate change law*, *op. cit.*, at 42.

143 J.E. Viñuales, "Due diligence in international environmental law", at 111, in H. Krieger, A. Peters, L. Kreuzer (eds), *Due diligence in the international legal order*, Oxford University Press, 2020, XVIII–402 p.

144 ECtHR, *Tătar v. Romania*, 27 January 2009, no 67021/01, § 120.

place under the state's jurisdiction, the establishment of a legal framework of anticipation for public and private persons, the cooperation and information of other states, the notification of the various risks, etc. This is what emerges in particular from the Advisory Opinion of the Chamber of the ITLOS on Seabed Disputes of 1 February 2011 on the *Responsibilities and obligations of States sponsoring persons and entities with respect to activities in the Area,*[145] even if the Tribunal followed rather convoluted and questionable reasoning.[146] This effect of precaution was also recognised by the Dutch court in the *Urgenda* case.[147] The latter had to assess The Netherlands' compliance with the duty of care in climate matters, which is provided for in the Dutch constitution and which largely corresponds to due diligence under international law. It considered that one of the main criteria that should guide it in this assessment is the principle of precaution. The due diligence standard then requires the state to use all reasonably available means to deal with the risk, which in practice implies, above all, asking what it would be unreasonable to expect of it in the circumstances of each case. This implies taking into account the means available to each state according to its own economic, social and geographical situation. Article 3 of the UNFCCC effectively refers to this criterion as follows: "... policies and measures to address climate change shall be cost-effective so as to ensure that overall benefits are achieved at the lowest possible cost. In order to achieve this goal, such policies and measures should take into account the diversity of socio-economic contexts ..." The aim is to identify the most efficient measures through a cost-benefit analysis. For example, in the context of global risks, it seems very difficult for a state to invoke an economic necessity in order not to apply these measures because of the proportionality rationale which tends to tip the balance towards the seriousness of the potential damage in a precautionary situation.

145 ITLOS, *Responsibilities and obligations of States sponsoring persons and entities with respect to activities in the Area* (*Request for Advisory Opinion submitted to the Seabed Disputes Chamber*), *op. cit.*, § 131.

146 Y. Kerbrat, S. Maljean-Dubois, "Les juridictions internationales et le principe de précaution, entre grande prudence et petites audaces", at 929, in *Unity and diversity of international law: essays in honour of Professor Pierre-Marie Dupuy*, Leiden, Martinus Nijhoff Publishers, 2014, XIV–1008 p.

147 The Hague District Court, *Urgenda Foundation v. State of the Netherlands*, *op. cit.*, §§ 4.56–4.63.

4.3 *Implementation of due Diligence Standards through the Complementarity of International and Domestic Norms*

International due diligence obligations related to global risks entail, as we have seen, the determination of the means of action at the domestic level. But the evaluation of the diligence – or negligence – of a state's action requires a standard of reference which can be found only in international norms, of both hard and soft law.

Most international climate obligations of states are obligations of means or due diligence obligations that require the use of all reasonably available means to achieve the common goal. Domestic courts often consider, for example, that the obligation periodically to re-evaluate NDCs and domestic law in the light of the latest scientific information available is an obligation of due diligence.[148] However, the implementation of states' climate commitments requires the identification of a standard of care as a reference by which to assess whether a state's action is sufficient. The elements of this standard are essentially to be found in the international norms themselves. In particular, the Katowice Rulebook for the Implementation of the Paris Agreement details the procedural obligations of states; it includes, for example, accounting guidelines and guidelines on the list of information to be reported on each NDC. In doing so, international law is integrated into national law in two ways: it limits and defines the extent of the state's discretion in the performance of its climate obligations, and it gives concrete content to the standard of diligence (or duty of care) expected of the state, including under its constitutional law. According to the Municipal Court of Prague, for instance, the standard of care to be taken into account results from the Constitution, the European Convention on Human Rights and the Paris Agreement, in particular its Article 4, §§ 13 and Article 14, relating to the elements that the state must take into account in establishing its NDC.[149]

The South African High Court has also indicated that national courts have to interpret domestic acts in accordance with international climate treaties because of the obligation to incorporate international law into domestic law.[150] The French Council of State has clearly recognised that international law is relevant to determining France's discretion[151] in relation to the execution of

148 See for instance United Kingdom, High Court of Justice, *R (oao Friends of the Earth) v. Secretary of State for Business Energy and Industrial Strategy*, 18 July 2022, §§ 277–278.

149 Prague Municipal Court, *Judgment No. 14A 101/2021*, 15 June 2022, § 228.

150 South Africa's High Court, *EarthLife Africa Johannesburg v. Minister of Environmental Affairs and Others, op. cit.*, § 83.

151 French Council of State, *Commune de Grande-Synthe v. France*, 19 November 2020, § 12.

its climate commitments, and the New Zealand High Court has also held that, while the Minister for Climate Change has discretion to determine the 2050 GHG emissions reduction target, this discretion is limited by international law, including the Intergovernmental Panel on Climate Change's reports.[152]

As already mentioned with regard to international law, the Dutch courts considered that the standard of diligence requires it to be demonstrated that the state was aware of the global risk caused by climate change – on this point domestic courts usually rely on the IPCC reports, which are considered to be the most legitimate means of evidence –, that it had control over the source of GHG emissions requiring it to act and that it did not diligently use the means reasonably available to it to achieve the objectives set.[153] In defining these different elements, international climate law provides valuable standards such as non-regression in the determination of the means constituted by NDCs (Article 3 of the Paris Agreement) or an evolving obligation of diligence that must be executed "as soon as possible" and with the "highest possible level of ambition" (Article 4 of the Paris Agreement).[154] Taking the interests of future generations and intergenerational equity into account is also based on international climate law.[155] Some due diligence standards may be even more specific, as is the case under the European Convention on Human Rights.[156] In the face of the global risk linked to climate change, it is therefore the articulation of hard and soft-law norms, of international as well as national or regional origin, that allows domestic courts to give effect to the international obligations of states related to the fight against climate change.

Due diligence obligations of states on the prevention of pandemics are also informed by international norms that must be used by domestic bodies when implementing them. Here again, domestic law must be interpreted in light of a due diligence standard deriving from international law. The International Health Regulations are a first source that provides criteria in this respect: Article 6 requires each state to assess events within its territory using an algorithm and to notify the WHO within 24 hours of any event that may constitute a public health emergency of international concern. The assessment of compliance with these obligations is based on a set of criteria that refers to a due diligence standard. The proof of negligence of the state is, first

152 High Court of New Zealand, *Thomson v. Minister for Climate Change Issues*, *op. cit.*, § 91.

153 The Hague District Court, *Urgenda Foundation v. State of the Netherlands*, *op. cit.*, §§ 4.63–4.66.

154 On this issue see J. Brunnée, "Procedure and substance in international environmental law", *Collected Courses of The Hague Academy of International Law*, vol. 405, 2020, at 201.

155 See for instance article 3 of the UNFCCC and the preamble of the Paris Agreement.

156 See The Hague Court of Appeals, *Urgenda Foundation v. State of the Netherlands*, 9 October 2018, § 42.

of all, the knowledge that it had of the existence of a global pandemic risk. With regard to the implementation of obligations to prevent the spread of the COVID-19 epidemic, for example, this knowledge had existed since the declaration of this type of health emergency by the Director General of the WHO on 30 January 2020, but some states, such as Italy, should have reacted as soon as suspected cases were identified even earlier. The second assessment criterion concerns the control exercised by the state over the risk to be prevented. Each state has at least some control over the risk of the spread of an epidemic on its territory in the light of its various prevention obligations. However, states may also be considered to have control over private actors, including companies, whose actions have an impact on this overall risk. As already noted, Article 24 of the International Health Regulations, for example, requires them to exercise control over operators of means of transport who are directly involved in preventing the spread of an epidemic.

Finally, as already mentioned, negligence is characterised by the failure to use reasonable means to address the risk. On a subjective point of view, the use of unreasonable means can first be ruled out in view of the circumstances in which a specific state found itself. Comparison with the behaviour of states in similar circumstances may also provide relevant clues. For example, as Italy was the first European country to be confronted with the spread of the COVID-19 epidemic, neighbouring states had its experience at their disposal in assessing the reasonableness of the health measures to be adopted. Similarly, the example of Taiwan and South Korea, whose diligence in containing the epidemic was remarkable, was not followed by many neighbouring states.[157] The second approach to assessing the reasonableness of states' actions is more objective, in that it relies on hard or soft-law instruments that give concrete form to the content of different obligations. For example, the WHO has developed a series of indicators for this purpose.[158] Similarly, in the event of a health emergency of international concern, the International Health Regulations allow the Director-General to make temporary recommendations to states to adapt health measures to the situation. Under the International Health Regulations, the deadline for implementation of the progressive obligations of Articles 5 and 13 was set for 2016, while Annex 1 provided for criteria in this regard.[159]

157 See J.E. Alvarez, "The WHO in the Age of Coronavirus", *AJIL*, 2020, at 583.

158 <https://www.who.int/ihr/IHR_Monitoring_Framework_Checklist_and_Indicators_fr.pdf>.

159 Annex 1 includes, e.g., core capacity requirements for surveillance and response, criteria for the assessment and notification of events that may constitute a public health emergency of international concern.

In a similar fashion, due diligence obligations related to the right to health are informed by standards set by international bodies such as the Committee on Economic, Social and Cultural Rights. In its General Observation n°14, the Committee thus indicated a series of criteria which must be followed by states parties to the Covenant when implementing these obligations in the domestic sphere. Concerning the obligation to develop a health system able to cope with pandemics, due diligence requires this interest to be mainstreamed in all public policies, a sufficiently large part of the national budget to be devoted to this issue, and the principle of non-regression to be followed … [160]

Guatemala Constitutional Court has ruled on an appeal against a decision of a supreme court ordering the state to provide sufficient supplies and equipment to healthworkers who were fighting COVID-19. The Constitutional Court dismissed the appeal on the grounds that Guatemala was in breach of several fundamental rights stemming from the constitution and many international treaties. In order to assess the diligence in the implementation of obligations related to the right to health regarding the availability, accessibility, non-discrimination and quality of medical goods and services in the context of a pandemic, it relied on the standard set by the CESCR in its General Observation no 14. Under criteria of progressiveness and non-regression, the Court found that states are compelled to take all means, within the limit of their resources, necessary progressively to attain the full realisation of the right to health. In view of the imminent risk posed by the COVID-19 virus, Guatemala had not sufficiently protected the right to health of medical workers.[161]

4.4 *In Search of due Diligence Standards for International Organisations*

As discussed above, it is difficult to find specific obligations to fight global risks for international organisations. Evelyne Lagrange identifies a possible auxiliary function of due diligence that would allow for the identification of particular obligations from the mandate of the organisation in certain circumstances.[162] However, any negligence would be more easily invoked against it by Member States than by other actors if its constituent instrument is limited to empowering it to act and does not compel it to do so. This may not be the case when the organisation imposes obligations on itself, for example by designating an organ to perform a specific task and thereby creating legitimate expectations to

160 CESCR, General Comment No 14 (2000), *op. cit.*, § 16.

161 Guatemala, Constitutional Court, 28 January 2021, Expediente 2758–2020, at 22.

162 E. Lagrange, "La responsabilité des organisations internationales pour violation d'une obligation de diligence", at 190, in SFDI, *Le standard de due diligence et la responsabilité internationale. Journée d'études franco-italienne du Mans*, Paris, Pedone, 2018, 340 p.

perform it. Some authors go further by proposing to look at the mandate of the organisation to establish possible negligence on its part, thus identifying obligations just by deriving them from its mandate.[163] The negligent omission is then taken into account as the result of a decision-making process, in the light of the specific circumstances of each case. Obligations to act can be linked to several elements of the mandate: risky activities of the international organisation; its favourable position to respond to a need; the fact that it benefits from an activity; the fact that it decides by itself to take on a specific role. The WHO, for example, recalled its central role in preventing and responding to pandemics in the resolution adopted by the World Health Assembly in spring 2020.[164] To define the WHO's mandate in relation to the outbreak and spread of a pandemic, it is necessary to identify its links with the risk of a pandemic in order to establish the control it could exercise over the situation and its possible negligence.[165] The source of this control does not necessarily have to be sought in formally binding instruments, but could also result in this case from the WHO's "epistemic authority"[166] with regard to the risk of a pandemic. This is the case first of all with regard to Member States: the Director-General is responsible for qualifying the public emergency as international in scope and for making temporary recommendations to prevent or reduce its spread. In the longer term in preparing for such a risk, the WHO can adopt strategies which, while not legally binding, have a strong influence on the domestic law and policy of its members. The WHO's control is also exercised over other international institutions with which it cooperates, in accordance with Article 14 of the International Health Regulations.[167] This issue has already arisen in relation to the Ebola epidemic in 2014, when WHO coordination with other stakeholders was almost

---

163 J. Klabbers, "Reflections on Role Responsibility: The Responsibility of International Organisations for Failing to Act", *EJIL*, 2018/4, at 1133.

164 World Health Assembly, Resolution WHA73.1, 19 May 2020.

165 ILA Study Group on Due Diligence in International Law, Second Report, July 2016, at 43.

166 On this notion see J. Klabbers, "The Normative Gap in International Organisations: the Case of the World Health Organisation", *International Organisations Law Review*, 2019/2, at 272–298.

167 "Cooperation of WHO with intergovernmental organisations and international bodies

1. WHO shall cooperate and coordinate its activities, as appropriate, with other competent intergovernmental organisations or international bodies in the implementation of these Regulations, including through the conclusion of agreements and other similar arrangements.
2. In cases in which notification or verification of, or response to, an event is primarily within the competence of other intergovernmental organisations or international bodies, WHO shall coordinate its activities with such organisations or bodies in order to ensure the application of adequate measures for the protection of public health.

non-existent.[168] The organisation also has an influence on the prevention of pandemic risk: it produces technical reports, recommendations to private and public research experts, and the annual World Health Report. All these indicators are used, for example, by the international financial institutions in their funding decisions for states. The WHO is necessarily a partner in global public health, including for some private actors; it thus exerts influence, particularly with regard to pharmaceutical companies and trans-carriers. It works with non-state actors on the gathering of health information related to emergencies in accordance with the International Health Regulations as revised in 2005. In defining these relationships, the WHO may set a standard of care for itself; the World Health Assembly, for example, has adopted a resolution specifying the procedure to be used for the diligent selection of non-state actors to work with the organisation.[169]

Once the organisation's mandate has been identified, it is possible to examine whether it has exercised it diligently by reference to a specific standard. First of all, the organisation must have knowledge of the existence of the global risk. Then, in order to assess the reasonableness of the actions of international organisations, Evelyne Lagrange proposes five components of a standard of care that would be specific to them.[170] First, a diligent organisation must have adequate procedures relating to its decision-making process so as not to make unreasonable decisions. In the case of the COVID-19 pandemic, many observers believe that the Director General of the WHO delayed too long in declaring a health emergency of international concern, probably for fear of overreaction by Member States. Second, a diligent organisation should have internal procedures for monitoring its decision-making processes. The WHO has no real accountability mechanism for evaluating its own action, the IHR Review Committee not seeming to be sufficient for this purpose.[171] Third, the organisation

3. Notwithstanding the foregoing, nothing in these Regulations shall preclude or limit the provision by WHO of advice, support, or technical or other assistance for public health purposes".

168 M. Eccleston-Turner, S. McArdle, R. Upshur, "Inter-Institutional Relationships in Global Health: Regulating Coordination and Ensuring Accountability", *Global health governance*, 2018, at 32. In the context of the COVID-19 pandemic, on 31 March 2020, the FAO, the WHO and the WTO adopted a joint statement on the adaptation of health measures in the face of other interests such as food security and trade, https://www.wto.org/french/news_f/news20_f/igo_26mar20_f.htm#:~:text=Le%2031%20mars%2C.

169 World Health Assembly, Resolution WHA 69.10, 28 May 2016, at 10.

170 E. Lagrange, "La responsabilité des organisations internationales pour violation d'une obligation de diligence", *op. cit.*, at 203–204.

171 G. Bartolini, "Are You Ready for a Pandemic? The International Health Regulations Put to the Test of Their "Core Capacity Requirements"", *EJIL: Talk!*, 1 June 2020.

is supposed to make reasonable use of the resources provided to it by its members. It is questionable in this case whether there were any shortcomings in the conduct of the international investigation into the origin of the pandemic. The World Health Assembly established an "Independent Evaluation of the WHO's COVID-19 Response" in May 2020.[172] Due to China's strong resistance, however, its experts were able to visit Wuhan only in January 2021 and their mandate was drastically limited. The WHO does not appear to have used all reasonable means to put pressure on China regarding the investigations.[173] Fourth, the organisation should "diligently consider the highest standard of behaviour"[174] before declaring that it does not have the capacity to act. Fifth, a diligent organisation should inform members of the risks to the people it is mandated to protect. During the COVID-19 pandemic, the WHO was at times very ambiguous about the measures adopted by states: for example, it congratulated the first to implement containment while insisting at the same time on the need to adopt measures that minimised interference with trade and freedom of movement.[175] The implementation of this kind of standard could, for example, without much difficulty lead to the recognition of the UN's responsibility for the spread of the cholera epidemic in Haiti by the Nepalese peacekeeping contingent after the earthquake of 2010.[176]

5 Conclusions

International law currently deals with the prevention of and the fight against global risks in a rather fragmented way. It provides for legal regimes devoted to one risk at a time which lack coordination with other legal regimes that

---

172 World Health Assembly, Resolution WHA73.1, 19 May 2020.

173 In the agreement with China it was established that the fact-finding mission would undertake to study only a limited number of working hypotheses defined in advance and on the basis of the preliminary results submitted by the state authorities, <https://www.lemonde.fr/planete/article/2021/01/07/la-chine-bloque-l-enquete-de-l-oms-sur- les-origines-du-sars-cov-2_6065473_3244.html>.

174 E. Lagrange, "La responsabilité des organisations internationales pour violation d'une obligation de diligence", *op. cit.*, at 203. My translation.

175 A. Von Bogdandy, P.A. Villareal, "International Law on Pandemic Response: A First Stocktaking in Light of the Coronavirus Crisis", *MPIL Research Paper Series*, n° 2020–07.

176 See for instance F. Mégret, "La responsabilité des Nations unies au temps du choléra", *RBDI*, 2013/1, at 170 ; M. Mondélice, "The UN and the Haiti cholera case: articulating the Rule of Law, immunities and responsibility of international organisations in international law", at 565–588, in S. Murase, S. Zhou (eds), *Epidemics and international law*, Leiden, Brill Nijhoff, 2021, XXXII–708 p.

have different objectives but that also have the capacity to produce effects on global risks. It has not yet really taken into account the global dimension of the threats posed by climate change and pandemics; it fails to capture the interplay between all the stakeholders and the rapidity of the evolution of risks.[177] An essential means of meeting the challenge of correctly addressing global risks is the integration principle, which first developed in international environmental law but is currently being transposed into other fields. This principle advocates that concerns related to global risks should be mainstreamed into all international and domestic state policies when activities are susceptible to having an impact on them. Even if it is just starting to be implemented, the integration approach provides a way to draw links between different levels of decision and different levels of norms which are all necessary to enable one efficiently to face global risks. This mainstreaming process requires to identify specific due diligence standards in the implementation of international obligations: what criteria must be followed in order to reduce GHG emissions or to carry out impact assessments or to establish a health system able to react to the outbreak of a pandemic? These standards are provided at the international level by both hard and soft-law instruments which state bodies – including courts – have to take into account in the elaboration and interpretation of domestic measures implementing international obligations. Thus, due diligence is used more and more in international law in order to pursue at least two objectives: to inform about action which has to be taken by several actors (private as well as public) at several levels – international, regional, domestic – and to reinforce state responsibility for the control of activities of other actors under their jurisdiction. This analysis could probably be transposed to other global risks, such as financial and cyber-risks. Indeed, international law tends to address them also in a fragmented way, through hard and soft-law instruments and by setting standards that must be implemented by the different stakeholders.[178]

177 On the shortcomings of international law in dealing with systemic risks see M.-A. Frison-Roche, "La responsabilité *ex-ante*", *Archives de philosophie du droit*, 2022, at 110.

178 See, among many publications, E. Fahey, *The EU as a global digital actor: institutionalising global data protection, trade, and cybersecurity*, Oxford, Hart Publishing, 2022, XXVIII–230 p.; U.A. Barton, *Rethinking regulation of international finance: law, policy and institutions*, Alphen aan den Rijn, Kluwer Law International, 2017, XVIII–256 p.

CHAPTER 3

Responsibilities for Global Risks

1 Introduction

International legal regimes of responsibility[1] have not been conceived to address the liability of the different actors involved in the fight against global risks, whether they be states, international organisations or private actors (2). While the conclusion could have been the inefficiency of responsibility in this context, the practice mainly before domestic courts shows that much litigation focuses on state responsibility for global risks, either through the invocation of breaches of human rights (3) or on the grounds of the violation of due diligence obligations of prevention of and reaction to these risks (4). A comparison of the multiple judicial decisions related to climate change and pandemics reveals the emergence of a "regime of responsibility for global risks" which could influence evolutions of international responsibility before international courts; some hints on this point may, for example, result from the advisory opinions on climate change state obligations currently under review by some of these courts (5).

2 The Limits of International Regimes of Responsibility

International rules of responsibility of states and of international organisations are not adapted to global risks: they do not address complex causation, attribution, shared responsibilities (mainly concurrent responsibilities), reparation of grave damage[2] ... Specific problems are related to the regime of the responsibility of international organisations, such as the difficulty in identifying specific obligations to be observed by the organisation.

1 For the purpose of this work, the terms "responsibility" and "liability" are used as synonyms. They are indeed clearly distinguished in English-speaking countries but not in several other legal traditions, and their use may be different in international law. See for instance S. Sucharitkul, "State Responsibility and International Liability Under International Law", *Loyola of Los Angeles International & Comparative Law Journal*, 1996, at 821.

2 See for instance C. Voigt, "State Responsibility for Climate Change Damages", *Nordic Journal of International Law*, 2008, at 1–22; M. Fitzmaurice, "Responsibility and climate change", *German Yearbook of International Law*, 2010, at 89–138.

 DOI:10.1163/9789004538702_005

The internationally wrongful acts of all the actors involved are distinct but interrelated, so it is difficult to consider them separately. The global risk of a pandemic, for example, implies cooperation between different "stakeholders" to avoid it and, after its occurrence, to address it and, speculatively, their multiple responsibilities. Climate change negative impacts are also provoked by the concurrence of a series of actions and omissions of several actors which contribute in different – but certain – ways to the final damage. International law for now does not directly address the responsibility of private actors, which is left to domestic law, even if the content of some of their obligations is contained in international law instruments.[3] In addition to this issue, the main shortfalls of the law of international responsibility relate to the complexity of the damage provoked by global risks (2.1), to the difficulty of the determination of causal links between the various acts or omissions and the damage (2.2), and to the ability to address the joint and several responsibility of the various actors involved (2.3).

2.1 *Multiplicity and Type of Damage Caused by Global Risks and Reparation*

One of the peculiarities of global risks consists in the width and variety of damage produced by their occurrence. These incidents of damage are diffuse both in time and space, and they affect multiple interests. Starting with pandemics, the most direct damage caused concerns life and health, including many people suffering the after-effects or secondary effects of the disease. However, pandemics also cause a great deal of damage in a more indirect way, in particular through the sanitary decisions taken by governments to limit their spread. The various containment measures, such as quarantine, lockdowns and border closures, cause widespread social and economic damage, to both states – which have to provide support for many economic activities – and individuals and to the various communities and populations affected.[4] In this sense, the global dimension of the damage caused by epidemics is clear. Regarding climate change, the IPCC 2014 report identifies all types of harms likely to be caused by this global risk. The extent of climate damage is thus determined by three components: climate events, risk exposure and vulnerability, which are all discussed in the IPCC reports.[5] As climate has an impact on the whole of the ecosystem balance

3 See, among many examples, the OECD Guidelines for Multinational Enterprises.

4 As shown by the example of the COVID-19 pandemic.

5 On this issue see C. Voigt, "Climate change and damages", at 465, in K.R. Gray, R. Tarasofsky, C. Carlarne (eds), *The Oxford handbook of international climate change law*, OUP, 2016, XXIV–822 p.

and on all human activities, negative effects of climate change affect natural elements such as oceans and land, but also a series of human rights (including the rights to life, food, health, cultural rights ...), economic activities etc.

The legal question is thus which damage could be compensated for and by what means in the context of the implementation of the responsibility of the states and international organisations involved. Some damage is purely individual, but several harms can be considered to be also collective because they are suffered either by the international community as a whole or, more specifically, by certain entities (peoples, indigenous populations, different groups, etc.).

The ILC's codification of international responsibility gives indications of the type of damage that entails reparation by states or by international organisations which have committed a wrongful act.[6] Possibly the subjects whose negligence is at the origin of the outbreak and spread of a pandemic or of the emission of GHGs would be required to make reparation for all the types of damage mentioned above, in accordance with international practice which, at least for state responsibility, is substantial. But the question is which categories of damage may be compensated for, also in relation to their specific victim. According to Article 33 of the Articles on Responsibility of States for Internationally Wrongful Acts, "1. The obligations of the responsible State ... may be owed to another State, to several States or to the international community as a whole, depending, inter alia, on the nature and content of the international obligation breached and the circumstances of the breach.

2. This Part is without prejudice to any right that may arise directly for the benefit of a person or entity other than a State as a result of the inter-State responsibility of the State".

First, the ILC expressly names as the collective entity entitled to reparation the international community – clearly affected by the negligence in preventing a pandemic or a climate risk. This is confirmed by the fact that many international prevention obligations are *erga omnes* obligations. In contrast, other entities and private persons are considered only under a "without prejudice" clause, so that the Commission has not attempted to define a specific legal regime of reparation for them, which would have been useful in particular in relation to collective damage. The possibility of reparation for this type of damage resulting, for example, from the violation of the right to health has nonetheless already been recognised in international practice.[7] The collective

6 Article 31 of the ARSIWA and article 31 of the ARIO.

7 The African Commission on Human and Peoples' Rights recognised Nigeria's violation of the Ogoni people's right to health and ordered specific remedies. ADHP Commission, *Social*

dimension of climate damage has also been highlighted by the Colombian Supreme Court: not only do all the inhabitants of this country suffer damage, but this is the case also of all the inhabitants of the planet as well as of the environment itself (purely ecological damage), and even of the Colombian Amazon, considered here as a subject of rights.[8] In the complaints before the Inter-American Commission on Human Rights, similarly, damage to the collective rights of certain indigenous people has been invoked[9] and the violation of the rights of the indigenous people from Torres Strait has been recognised by the Human Rights Committee.[10]

Although compensation could conceivably be used as a means of redress for the material and moral damage caused by a pandemic or by the negative effects of climate change, the commitment to liability for this type of global risk is largely aimed at restoring legality, i.e. compliance with violated obligations. The most relevant secondary norms would thus be reparation in the form of satisfaction, as well as two types of secondary obligations other than reparation – cessation and guarantees of non-repetition. For example, states should cease to violate their obligations to build a health system capable of dealing with such emergencies by providing it with adequate funding. Or, since the risk of occurrence of repeated negligence is high, the WHO should, for example, change its procedures and implement effective investigations to determine the origin of a pandemic. This approach would fit the integral (non-reciprocal) nature of most epidemic prevention obligations, as is confirmed by Article 48 of the ARSIWA which allows a "non-injured" state to claim reparation "in the interest of the beneficiaries of the obligation breached".[11]

---

and economic rights action centre and Centre for economic and social rights v. Nigeria, 13–27 October 2001, No 155/96.

8 Supreme Court of Colombia, *Future Generations v. Ministry of the Environment and Others*, *op. cit.*, at 45.

9 See for instance the *Petition to the Inter-American Commission on Human Rights Seeking Relief from Violations of the Rights of Arctic Athabaskan Peoples Resulting from Rapid Arctic Warming and Melting Caused by Emissions of Black Carbon by Canada,* filed on the 23 April 2013.

10 Human Rights Committee, *Daniel Billy and others v. Australia* (*Torres Strait Islanders Petition*), Views adopted by the Committee under article 5 (4) of the Optional Protocol, concerning communication No. 3624/2019, CCPR/C/135/D/3624/2019.

11 "Invocation of responsibility by a State other than an injured State

1. Any State other than an injured State is entitled to invoke the responsibility of another State in accordance with paragraph 2 if:
   (a) the obligation breached is owed to a group of States including that State, and is established for the protection of a collective interest of the group; or
   (b) the obligation breached is owed to the international community as a whole.

2.2 *Complex Causality*

The main pitfall in considering the content of responsibility for global risks is the establishment of a causal link between negligence and damage. Two types of causal links are concerned: general ("factual causation") and specific ("proximate causation"). As for general causation, the spread of a contagious pathogen is clearly related to the outbreak of epidemics. In the same way, GHG emissions are now firmly linked to the main current climate changes – mainly thanks to the IPCC's work. But specific causality – between a particular act or omission and a particular harm – is very difficult to prove.

One of the main characteristics of pandemic and climate change risk liability is indeed that the final damage is produced by an accumulation, in space and in time, of acts and omissions. However, the ILC's work on responsibility considers this type of situation only to a very limited extent. The Commission generally relies on the principle of the independence of responsibility: each subject is responsible only for his own act. It has nevertheless included the hypothesis of a plurality of responsible actors in Article 47 of the ARSIWA and in Article 48 of the Articles on the Responsibility of International Organisations (ARIO). This case is, however, taken into consideration in a very restrictive way, since the different subjects involved should be at the origin of the same internationally wrongful act, thereby engaging their joint and several liability or possibly their subsidiary liability. However, in the case of a pandemic or of climate change, a plurality of actors is not the cause of joint liability – *stricto sensu* – stemming from a single wrongful act, but of concurrent liability when the damage is caused by an accumulation of several internationally wrongful acts. The determination of the content of liability then requires one to analyse the concurrent causes of the damage and to establish the various adequate causal links in order to determine the contribution of each actor to the final damage. In the present case, two types of links could be taken into consideration: complementary causality – each wrongful act having contributed to the damage in a certain proportion, which requires apportionment of

---

2. Any State entitled to invoke responsibility under paragraph 1 may claim from the responsible State:
   (a) cessation of the internationally wrongful act, and assurances and guarantees of non-repetition in accordance with article 30; and
   (b) performance of the obligation of reparation in accordance with the preceding articles, in the interest of the injured State or of the beneficiaries of the obligation breached.
3. The requirements for the invocation of responsibility by an injured State under articles 43, 44 and 45 apply to an invocation of responsibility by a State entitled to do so under paragraph 1".

the obligation to make reparation for it – and cumulative causality, according to which the damage could have arisen only from the accumulation of internationally wrongful acts, which implies that one must seek a criterion of apportionment of reparation.[12] However, the establishment of these causal links depends largely on the content of each preventive obligation, so that the more distant in time or space the breach of the obligation is from the damage, the more difficult it is to identify the causal link.

Violation by states of certain obligations of result, such as obligations to inform about the occurrence of suspicious health events or obligations to implement a climate impact assessment, can be linked without much difficulty to the damage caused by the outbreak of a pandemic or by some specific polluting activities. Similarly, negligence in the application of obligations of means involving the adoption of immediate measures to contain a health emergency on the part of states can be linked without great difficulty to a number of harms directly caused by them; this is, for example, the case with states which do not follow the procedures instituted by the International Health Regulations. But the further one moves away from the territory of a state the more difficult it is to establish this link. At the beginning of the COVID-19 pandemic, for example, the negligence of the United States or Brazil has certainly caused serious harm to the people on their territory.[13] But should they also be considered as the cause of health damage in the region in which they are located? Establishing a causal link between the GHG emissions against which the state is supposed to act and a specific harm is also extremely difficult. The diffuse nature of these emissions makes it impossible to identify their link with a specific harm. The assessment is even more complex when the state is accused of violating its obligation to prevent possible damage, as the latter has not yet occurred.

With regard to progressive obligations, the further back in time we go in relation to the outbreak and spread of a pandemic, the more complex it is to establish a causal link between negligence and damage. The failure of many states to meet their obligation to build up a health system capable of responding to this type of emergency and to detect this type of risk at an early stage

12 S. Besson, "La responsabilité solidaire des États et/ou des organisations internationales: une institution négligée", at 121–159, in A. Supiot (ed.), *Face à l'irresponsabilité : la dynamique de la solidarité*, Paris, Collège de France, 2018, 182 p.

13 On the different measures adopted by states to cope with the pandemic, see the database *COVID tracking project*, <https://COVIDtracking.com/data/national>.

could be seen, for example, as one of the causes of the COVID-19 pandemic, but the burden of proof appears to be particularly high.

The same type of difficulty is encountered in establishing the causal link between the possible negligence of international organisations and the identified damage. The slowness in declaring a public health emergency of international concern on the part of the WHO's Director General or in deciding to send a fact-finding mission to China during the COVID-19 pandemic, for example, may have effectively contributed to aggravating its effects. It is more difficult to link the lack of accountability procedures at the WHO to the resulting damage.

2.3 *Joint and Several Liability*

Full compensation for the overall damage caused by the realisation of global risks requires the ability to take into account the competing responsibilities of the different actors involved. The system of joint and several liability would best correspond to the complex causality resulting from the multiplicity of responsibilities of the subjects whose negligence contributes to the outbreak and spread of a pandemic or to the negative effects of climate change: it avoids victims receiving only a part of the compensation due to them and it also avoids the unjust enrichment of some of the responsible actors. Moreover, it corresponds to the fact that in this case several of the subjects who may be liable have violated the same type of obligation. The secondary obligations of reparation could thus best correspond to the characteristics of the primary obligations violated, as required by regimes of international responsibility.[14]

While it is not necessary to determine the specific share of each act in causing the damage at the stage of liability, it seems essential to consider it when one wishes to assess the amount of compensation.[15] The Dutch District Court, for example, stated in the *Urgenda* case that "emission reduction therefore concerns both a joint and individual responsibility of the signatories to the UN Climate Change Convention".[16] Most of the time, however, national courts do not have to deal with a possible allocation – or reduction – of the burden

---

14 This can be inferred from the link between articles 35 (Restitution) and 36 (Compensation) of the ARSIWA, according to which full reparation must first be sought through the re-establishment of the situation that existed before the commission of the internationally wrongful act and compensation is due only insofar as the damage cannot be repaired through restitution.

15 S. Maljean-Dubois, "La responsabilité internationale de l'Etat pour les dommages climatiques", at 210, in C. Cournil, L. Varison, M. Delmas-Marty (eds), *Les procès climatiques: entre le national et l'international*, Paris, Pedone, 2018, 300 p.

16 The Hague District Court, *Urgenda Foundation v. State of the Netherlands, op. cit.*, § 4.79.

of reparation, in particular because they are asked to order the state to comply with its international obligations.[17]

As it stands, however, the regime of joint and several liability as envisaged by the ILC does not seem applicable to the case of liability for global risks. In accordance with Article 47 of ARSIWA and Article 48 of ARIO, the prohibition of unjust enrichment seems to make it impossible to cumulate actions against the different actors. In practice, most international courts address competing liabilities separately, imposing full reparation of the damage on an actor, often on the ground of equivalence of conditions, or at least of the indivisibility of the damage. On the basis of this observation, an academic study considers a series of principles for the interpretation of the rules of international responsibility, allowing the implementation of joint and several liability in the case of shared responsibility.[18] Principle 4 corresponds precisely to the situation of a pandemic or of climate change:[19] "[i]nternational persons share responsibility for multiple internationally wrongful acts when each of them engages in separate conduct consisting of an action or omission that:

(a) is attributable to each of them separately; and
(b) constitutes a breach of an international obligation for each of those international persons; and
(c) contributes to the indivisible injury of another person".

As regards reparation, joint and several liability would imply that "each international person sharing responsibility is under an obligation to make full reparation for the indivisible injury caused by the single or multiple internally wrongful acts, unless its contribution to the injury is negligible",[20] which would be accompanied by the possibility of recourse on the part of the subject who

17 D.H. Cole, "The problem of shared responsibility in international climate law", at 290, in A. Nollkaemper, D. Jacobs (eds), *Distribution of responsibilities in international law*, Cambridge University Press, 2015, XXIV–448 p.

18 A. Nollkaemper, J. D'Aspremont, C. Ahlborn, B. Boutin, N. Nedeski, I. Plakokefalos, "Guiding Principles on Shared Responsibility in International Law", *EJIL*, 2020/1, at 15–72.

19 It is a case of "cumulative responsibility" in the words of A. Nollkaemper, D. Jacobs, "Introduction: mapping the normative framework for the distribution of shared responsibility", p. 1, in A. Nollkaemper, D. Jacobs (eds), *Distribution of responsibilities in international law*, Cambridge University Press, 2015, XXIV–448 p.

20 Principle 10.

has fully repaired the damage.[21] While these principles are compelling,[22] they still need to be confirmed by international practice.[23]

Michael Faure and André Nollkaemper have also proposed using principles of law and economics to award the victims compensation which is proportional to the damage determined according to the probability of causality.[24] In this case, it is ultimately the criterion of control that seems to be decisive in the allocation of the reparation obligation: the degree of effective control would then determine the share of responsibility attributed to each responsible actor. Other authors propose, in regard to climate change, either the setting up of joint and several liability leading to the objective responsibility of direct polluters, or compelling GHG emitters to contribute to a common fund intended to combat climate change.[25] These issues imply seeking innovative means of redress, while relying on the principles of international responsibility.

These challenges to international regimes of responsibility are closely related to the peculiarities of global risks. Paul Ricoeur, for example, insists on the fact that the reversal of the relationship between Man and Nature raises questions in terms of responsibility which is now understood more as a limit to human power than as a means of redress for a wrongful act.[26] In the same vein, Hans Jonas considers that power and danger lead to a wider responsibility, well

21 Principle 12.

22 But see the limits of implementation identified by D.H. Cole, "The problem of shared responsibility in international climate law", at 290, in A. Nollkaemper, D. Jacobs (eds), *Distribution of responsibilities in international law*, Cambridge University Press, 2015, XXIV–448 p.

23 Even if international courts sometimes affirm the existence of this kind of responsibility. E.g., the ITLOS Seabed Disputes Chamber has held that several sponsoring states may incur joint and several liability when they contribute to a common loss, *Responsibilities and obligations of States sponsoring persons and entities with respect to activities in the Area (Request for Advisory Opinion submitted to the Seabed Disputes Chamber)*, *op. cit.*, § 201. The CESCR seems to refer to a joint and several responsibility of members of the international community to cooperate in dealing with disasters in case of emergency and to address the problem of transmissible diseases, CESCR, General Comment No 14 (2000), *op. cit.*, § 40.

24 M.G. Faure, A. Nollkaemper, "International liability as an instrument to prevent and compensate for climate change", *Stanford journal of international law*, 2007, at 164.

25 J. Viñuales, "La distribution de la charge de protéger l'environnement: expressions juridiques de la solidarité", at 19–36, in A. Supiot (ed.), *Face à l'irresponsabilité: la dynamique de la solidarité*, Paris, Collège de France, 2018, 182 p.

26 P. Ricoeur, "Postface", at 251–261, in F. Lenoir (ed.), *Le temps de la responsabilité. Entretiens sur l'éthique*, Paris, Fayard, 1991, 272 p.

beyond intersubjective relationships.[27] According to some observers, in conclusion, "the limited relevance of state responsibility law to some emerging global problems has become visible".[28]

This "crisis of responsibility" is due to the renewal of the links between risk, responsibility and power leading to the "organised irresponsibility" identified by Ulrich Beck which is the result of the impossibility of attributing wrongful acts to anyone in regard to global risks.[29]

2.4 *Relationship between the Liability of International Organisations and the Liability of Member States*

In the absence of a sufficiently developed regime of joint and several liability, the rules of international responsibility as codified by the ILC allow one to consider the possible responsibility of member states for the negligence committed by an international organisation in regard to global risks. However, this possibility is exceptional, the principle being the non-liability of states as members of the organisation. First of all, the Commission addresses, in Article 61 of the ARIO, the hypothesis of circumvention of an obligation by member states of an international organisation. This scenario is not well suited to liability in the context of global risks because it requires an intentional criterion revealed by active conduct, whereas in this case liability rests mainly on the passivity of the actors involved.

On the other hand, two categories of subsidiary liability can be identified, in accordance with Article 48[30] of the ARIO. First, the exceptional responsibility of member states could be sought when it is impossible to hold the international

27 H. Jonas, *The imperative responsibility. In search for an ethics for the technological age*, The University of Chicago Press, 1984, XII–256 p.

28 K. Creutz, *State responsibility in the international legal order: a critical appraisal*, Cambridge University Press, 2020, at 3.

29 A. Giddens, "Risk and responsibility", *op. cit.*, at 8.

30 "Responsibility of an international organisation and one or more States or international organisations

1. Where an international organisation and one or more States or other international organisations are responsible for the same internationally wrongful act, the responsibility of each State or organisation may be invoked in relation to that act.
2. Subsidiary responsibility may be invoked insofar as the invocation of the primary responsibility has not led to reparation.
3. Paragraphs 1 and 2:
   (a) do not permit any injured State or international organisation to recover, by way of compensation, more than the damage it has suffered;
   (b) are without prejudice to any right of recourse that the State or international organisation providing reparation may have against the other responsible States or international organisations".

organisation accountable. It could be considered that states have failed in a due diligence obligation to ensure that the organisation is provided with the means necessary for the proper performance of its mission or, at least, not to deprive it of those means. This reasoning would be valid when the organisation's processes make its decisions largely dependent on member states, leaving it powerless in the face of their inaction.[31] For example, in view of the WHO's shortcomings in the management of the Ebola epidemic in 2014, member states could be held alternatively responsible for the major budget cuts decided for the activities of the emergency department shortly before the outbreak of the epidemic.[32] The same question could be asked about various decisions taken by WHO member states in the years preceding the COVID-19 pandemic and, in particular, about the insufficient reinforcement of its resources when the IHR were revised. But this possible best efforts obligation of Member States in their participation in the WHO has very little basis in practice. A second possibility could be to rely on Article 40, § 2[33], of the ARIO to hold member states subsidiarily liable for the organisation's failure to fulfil its secondary obligation to make reparation for the damage it has caused, in the absence of an adequate mechanism. This rationale is used, for example, by the European Court of Human Rights, which considers that the member states of an international organisation bear subsidiary responsibility when the latter does not ensure protection of fundamental rights equivalent to that required by the European Convention on Human Rights,[34] thereby putting pressure on states to develop such protection mechanisms within the international organisations of which they are members. However, this possibility does not help to take into account international organisations' responsibility in cases of negligence.

Even if these obstacles could be overcome, there is still a major stumbling block with regard to the content of the responsibility of international organisations. It is conceivable that the competing responsibilities of states and of international organisations could be called into question at both state and international levels. Numerous lawsuits have already been filed in domestic courts against states for their negligence in preventing and responding to

31 See for instance, in regard to the right to health, CESCR, General Comment No 14 (2000), *op. cit.*, § 39.

32 On this issue see M. Eccleston-Turner, S. McArdle, R. Upshur, "Accountability, International Law, and the World Health Organisation: A need for Reform?", *op. cit.*

33 "The members of a responsible international organisation shall take all the appropriate measures that may be required by the rules of the organisation in order to enable the organisation to fulfil its obligations under this Chapter".

34 See for instance, ECtHR, *Al-Dulimi and Montana Management Inc. v. Switzerland*, 21 June 2016, no 5809/08.

the COVID-19 pandemic, for example. The possibility of the parallel liability of states and international organisations in this kind of situation has already been recognised by both international and state courts.[35] International organisations could be held accountable for the same negligence both according to their extra-contractual responsibility before domestic courts and on the ground of their international responsibility. But several major pitfalls may be identified: first of all, domestic courts would be opposed to the organisation's immunities from jurisdiction; then arises the question of the determination of the liability regime in the event that the organisation has caused damage to private actors. When the extra-contractual responsibility of the organisation is called into question, the legal regime to be applied could either be based on international law or determined by resorting to principles of conflicts of laws and jurisdictions.[36] The codification of the International Law Commission does not provide any real guidance on this subject.

But, despite such realistic statements on the limits of international responsibility regimes, other forms of responsibility are, on the other hand, much used in the fight against global risks, and the practice related to them could give insights into the possibilities of the evolution of international responsibility, following the path opened by the studies on shared responsibility.

3 Responsibility for Global Risks Based on Violations of Human Rights

State responsibility for violation of human rights obligations can be invoked before both domestic and international courts. Several human rights are threatened by global risks, thus the "human rights turn" of litigation is a way of linking the domestic and the international levels of responsibility and to ensure that victims have standing before courts and tribunals in order to obtain reparation. While this is a common feature of pandemic and climate litigation, the relationship of each climate risk with human rights breaches is somewhat different. On one hand, an infringement of the right to health is directly connected to the failure to prevent the pandemic risk (3.1). On the

35 See for instance, Hague Appeals Court, *Stichting Mothers of Srebrenica et al. v. The Netherlands*, Case no C/09/295247, 16 July 2014; The Netherlands Supreme Court, *Nuhanovic v. the Dutch State*, Case no 12/03324, 6 September 2013; ECtHR, *Stichting mothers of Srebrenica and others v. The Netherlands*, 11 June 2013, no 65542/12.

36 On this issue see, e.g., M. Forteau, "Régime général de responsabilité ou *lex specialis*?", *RBDI*, 2013/1, at 147.

other hand, insufficient climate action may lead to the more indirect violation of several human rights (3.2).

3.1 *Responsibility for the Pandemic Risk Directly Related to the Right to Health*

As we have seen, states have several obligations to prevent epidemics stemming from the right to health; it is thus possible to try to ground their responsibility on the breach of this human right, as well at the international and national levels. Several claimants, for example, have challenged the insufficient protection of their health by states in the context of the COVID-19 pandemic – through the right to life – before the European Court of Human Rights.[37] The Committee on Economic, Social and Cultural Rights issued two statements, in 2020 and in 2021, to remind states parties to the Covenant of their obligations linked to the right to health in terms of accessibility and equitable distribution of vaccines against COVID-19, which breach could give rise to individual communications before the Committee.[38] Obligations related to the right to health include not only domestic policies but also international action. The UN Special Rapporteur on the right to the highest attainable standard of health has, for example, issued a report on Sweden, including comments on its obligations in relation to the right to health in its development assistance policies in Uganda and within the international financial institutions this state is a member of. In 2003 the Special Rapporteur also addressed the influence of WTO agreements (in particular TRIPS) on the right to health. When intellectual property rights exclude people from access to medicines because of high prices, there may be a violation of the right to health. He considered various international trade-related obligations of states, including the need to carry out a right to health impact assessment of proposed new agreements and to avoid "TRIPS-plus" clauses if they are likely to infringe the right to health. The Special Rapporteur, for instance, has adopted a press release on the trade agreement between the United States and Peru which included such clauses in 2005 in order to ask states parties to take the right to health into account in this treaty.[39]

---

37 See, e.g., ECtHR, *Le Mailloux v. France*, 5 November 2020, no 18108/20.

38 Statement on universal and equitable access to vaccines for the coronavirus disease (COVID-19), 15 December 2020, E/C.12/2020/2 and Statement on universal affordable vaccination against coronavirus disease (COVID-19), international cooperation and intellectual property, 23 April 2021, E/C.12/2021/1.

39 J. Bueno de Mesquita, P. Hunt, R. Khosla, "The Human Rights Responsibility of International Assistance and Cooperation in Health", at 116–127, in M. Gibney, S. Skogly (eds), *Universal Human Rights and Extraterritorial Obligations*, Philadelphia, University of Pennsylvania Press, 2010, 256 p.

Several claims based on insufficient action and the negligence of states in the prevention of the damage caused by the COVID-19 pandemic have been submitted to national courts of multiple states. In most cases, claimants allege the violation of the right to health under both constitutional and international rules. Some of these complaints concern specifically the inadequate protection of health workers. In one of these cases brought before a Mexican court, the judges examined the scope of international obligations of states related to the right to health. The court thus held that there was an obligation on health authorities to prevent the spread of COVID-19 and to protect the health of medical staff.[40] In a similar case, the Constitutional Court of Guatemala not only relied on the right to health as provided by several international treaties, but also on the interpretation of state obligations in General Observation No 14 of the Committee on Economic, Social and Cultural Rights.[41]

3.2 *Responsibility for Climate Change Indirectly Related to Several Human Rights*

A priori, the various obligations under the international legal regime for combating climate change do not create rights that are directly addressed to individuals. On a reading of the UNFCCC, the Kyoto Protocol and the Paris Agreement, and whatever the criteria used to determine the possibility of relying directly on their provisions – which vary according to each state – it would appear that the authors of these treaties intended to create obligations solely between states parties, with the latter being responsible for adopting the obligations enforceable against states or GHG emitters by private actors in their respective legal systems. This was the conclusion reached, for instance, by the Hague District Court in the *Urgenda* case, when the applicant intended to invoke these instruments directly in support of its claim.[42]

However, most plaintiffs in such cases – before both domestic and international courts – have chosen to invoke international human rights law as well to challenge the failure of states to act in this area. The climate responsibility of states is thus more and more frequently recognised for the violation of their obligations to protect human rights, which for the most part appear without much difficulty among the international standards directly invocable by private individuals.

While many international bodies – in particular within the framework of the United Nations – have in recent years begun to work on the links between

40 Mexico, Sixth District Court of the State of Sinaloa, 10 May 2021, Case No. 208/2020-3B.

41 Guatemala, Constitutional Court, 28 January 2021, Expediente 2758–2020.

42 The Hague District Court, *Urgenda Foundation v. State of the Netherlands*, *op. cit.*, 4.42.

the fight against climate change and the protection of human rights,[43] the central issue in litigation is to establish a sufficient causal link between the state's failure to combat climate change and the risks of human rights violations. Several international courts and treaty bodies have recognised this link. In particular, the Inter-American Court of Human Rights, in an advisory opinion of 15 November 2017, stressed on the one hand that the right to a healthy environment in itself constitutes an internationally protected fundamental right (whether enshrined in texts or in case law) and on the other hand that several human rights are particularly vulnerable with regard to the adverse effects of climate change. This second category includes in particular the rights to life, security, health, water and property.[44] The European Court of Human Rights has also held that the failure of states to act to protect the environment, including in cases of doubt about the adverse effects of an activity (thus using the precautionary principle), may amount to a violation of the right to private life and of the protection of the home.[45] The ECTHR recognises not only the existence of numerous obligations to prevent damage to a healthy environment in this context, but also the possible imminent breaches – not yet realised, by definition – if the interest in question is at serious risk of violation.[46]

Some UN human rights committees have also had the opportunity to address this issue. The Committee on the Rights of the Child, for example, while rejecting a claim against several states parties as inadmissible, still held that states are legally responsible for the harmful effects of GHG emissions originating in their territory on children outside their borders when they exercise effective control over the sources of pollution. It considered that states' failure to act

43 C. Cournil, C. Perruso, "Réflexions sur "l'humanisation" des changements climatiques et la "climatisation" des droits de l'Homme. Émergence et pertinence", *op. cit.*

44 Inter-American court of human rights, *Environment and human rights*, advisory opinion OC-23/17 of November 15, 2017. Similarly, the Committee on the Elimination of Discrimination against Women, in its General Recommendation No 37, has advised States Parties on how to fulfil their obligations to mitigate and adapt to climate change, while respecting the rights protected by the Convention, and highlighted the particular vulnerability of women's rights in disaster situations. CEDAW, General Recommandation no 37, 7 February 2018, CEDAW/C/GC/37.

45 According to the ECtHR, "despite the absence of a causal probability in the present case, the existence of a serious and substantial risk to the applicants' health and well-being placed a positive obligation on the state to adopt reasonable and adequate measures capable of protecting the rights of the persons concerned to respect for their private life and their home and, more generally, to enjoy a healthy and protected environment", *Tătar v. Romania, op. cit.*, § 107. My translation.

46 ECtHR, *Di Sarno and others v. Italy*, 10 January 2012, no. 30765/08. See also R.H.J. Cox, "The liability of European States for climate change", *Utrecht Journal of International and European Law*, 2014, at 125–135.

threatens several children's rights, among which are the rights to life, health, and culture.[47] In the *Torres Strait Islanders* case, the Human Rights Committee found that Australia's failure to protect the rights to the culture, life and private life of indigenous people by taking adaptation measures constituted a breach of the Covenant.[48]

Several domestic courts have ruled on the violation of subjective rights linked to the climate obligations of states. This relationship is considered basically in two different ways. First and less frequently, some courts tend to derive subjective rights directly from international climate law. The Supreme Court of Brazil, for example, faced with an appeal for violation of a fundamental domestic rule, had to examine the government's failure to finance a climate fund as a violation of the constitutional right to an ecologically balanced environment. It took the opportunity to indicate that environmental law treaties are a special type of human rights treaties which have supra-legislative status under Brazilian constitutional law. Therefore, any Brazilian law or decree that contradicts the Paris Agreement, including the nationally determined contribution as an implementation measure of this treaty, may be invalidated. Any action or omission contrary to this protection is thus considered as a direct violation of constitutional rights. The main consequence of the duty to mitigate climate change in the light of Brazil's international commitments is the constitutional obligation to allocate the funds provided for in an effective manner.[49] The Municipal Court of Prague, in an action concerning the illegality of a violation of fundamental rights by an administrative authority, held that the right to a favourable environment is based on the Constitution, the European Convention on Human Rights and, more surprisingly, the Paris Agreement. It concluded that the government's failure to combat climate change in violation of the Paris Agreement also constitutes a breach of the applicants' right to a favourable environment.[50]

Secondly, and more frequently, domestic courts consider that the existence of a healthy environment – which is a subjective right in itself – is also necessary for the exercise of many other fundamental rights, and that international climate law contributes to setting out the conditions that should allow this exercise. The link between this legal regime and subjective rights is thus more indirect. The Colombian Supreme Court, seised of a constitutional appeal for

---

47 Committee on the Rights of the Child, *Sacchi, et al. v. Argentina et al.*, *op. cit.*

48 Human Rights Committee, *Daniel Billy and others v. Australia* (*Torres Strait Islanders Petition*), *op. cit.*

49 Brazilian Supreme Court, *PSB et al v Brazil* (*on Climate Fund*), 1 July 2022, § 30.

50 Prague Municipal Court, *Judgment No. 14A 101/2021*, *op. cit.*, § 327.

tutela, considered that the existence of a healthy environment is indispensable for the exercise of several human rights, including those of future generations. The failure of the Colombian authorities to implement their NDC under the obligations of the Paris Agreement, including the prohibition of deforestation, constitutes a violation of these rights.[51] The Court of Appeal of The Hague considered that the "duty of care" requiring the Netherlands to respect their obligations under the climate treaties is based not only on the Constitution, but also on Articles 2 and 8 of the European Convention on Human Rights, which claimants can directly rely on and which have supra-legislative authority in Dutch law. The Court thus considered that non-compliance with the Paris Agreement also constituted a violation of subjective rights under the European Convention.[52] In the same vein, a Belgian court has held that the state's inaction in the face of climate change breached the plaintiffs' human rights based on Articles 2 and 8 of the European Convention, in addition to other obligations contained in the Civil Code.[53]

While strategical litigation against states on global risks through human rights implementation is rather favourable in terms of the possibility for claimants to rely directly on these rights, it nonetheless has some flaws. This perspective is indeed usually focused on the individual dimension of responsibility rather than on collective action, which is a necessity when facing global risks. This is one of the reasons explaining the recent multiplication of domestic litigation on the insufficiency of state action against global risks before national courts beyond mere human rights issues.

4 State Responsibility for the Breach of International Norms on Global Risks before Domestic Courts

Domestic courts participate in the enforcement of international law, including primary and secondary rules,[54] in various ways, thus giving "indirect" or "reflex" effect to it. This is evident in the climate field but also in part in health litigation.

51 Supreme Court of Colombia, *Future Generations v. Ministry of the Environment and Others*, *op. cit.*, at 13.

52 The Hague Court of Appeals, *Urgenda Foundation v. State of the Netherlands*, *op. cit.*, § 69.

53 Brussels Court of First Instance, *vzw Klimaatzaak v. Kingdom of Belgium & Others*, 17 June 2021, at 83.

54 According to the distinction introduced in the work of the ILC on the international responsibility of states by Roberto Ago, *Yearbook of the ILC*, 1973, vol. II, at 176.

The contribution of national courts to the effectiveness of state responsibility for breaches of international rules on global risks depends on many domestic factors such as the incorporation of international norms into national law, the rank of international norms, the definition of the standing of individual claimants, the act of state doctrine, the conditions for direct reliance on international treaties, the methods of interpretation of international norms, the rules for resolving conflicts of international obligations, etc.[55] Despite great differences between domestic legal orders on these issues, a high number of claims against states' inaction regarding global risks are introduced before national courts all over the world. These courts are more and more willing to retain state responsibility by taking into account the breach of international rules on global risks, thus giving effect to these primary rules as well as to the secondary rules of international responsibility, although indirectly.

From the point of view of international law, the question of the responsibility of a state to private actors, as we have seen,[56] has not been addressed by the International Law Commission, which has, however, formulated a "without prejudice" clause in Article 33, § 2, of the ARSIWA: "[t]his Part is without prejudice to any right which the international responsibility of a State may create directly for the benefit of a person or entity other than a State". There is therefore nothing to prevent an individual, as a matter of principle, from invoking such responsibility. The application of customary international rules on state responsibility by domestic courts then depends, logically, on the possibilities left by each national legal order. Domestic litigation thus shows that, by ruling on state responsibility and ordering governments to take effective measures to address global risks, national courts contribute to the implementation of climate and health obligations (4.1). In regard to situations in which negative effects of global risks have already occurred, domestic courts may also indirectly contribute to the implementation of secondary rules of international responsibility (4.2).

4.1 *Contribution to the Effectiveness of Primary Obligations of States*

Domestic courts address this question in different ways in the fields of climate change and pandemics. As we have seen, state responsibility for global risks is often grounded on human rights violations. But the effectiveness of climate law can also result, indirectly, from rules considered by courts only as

55 E. Lagrange, "L'efficacité des normes internationales concernant la situation des personnes privées dans les ordres juridiques internes", *Collected Courses of The Hague Academy of International Law*, vol. 356, 2012, at 321.

56 Cf *supra*, Chapter 3, 2.

modifying the situation of individuals: the rules of international climate law are most often not considered as creating subjective rights which individuals could directly rely on, but are likely to affect their situation – in particular if they are not implemented – including for future generations. On this basis, a national court may agree to give effect to them in litigation, in particular to prevent serious and irreversible damage. Whatever the means chosen to achieve this result, almost all judges insist on the global nature of the issue which justifies a particular approach on their part, as well as on the possibility for domestic judicial bodies, alongside the legislative and executive bodies, to contribute to the effectiveness of the state's international obligations.[57] The German Federal Constitutional Court heard an appeal against the Climate Act on the ground that it did not provide a sufficiently definite timeline for its enforcement and that it would thus have left an excessive burden on future generations, thereby jeopardising their exercise of many fundamental rights. According to the Court, Article 20a[58] of the Basic Law, which compels the state to take action to protect the climate, includes an international dimension, since this issue can be resolved only at the global level. The conclusion and ratification of the Paris Agreement are precisely a means of implementing this constitutional obligation: "[t]he fact that the Paris target is explicitly named as the basis of Germany's Federal Climate Change Act is closely related to the obligation to take climate action arising from Art. 20a GG. Due to the genuinely global dimension of climate change, the State can ultimately achieve the objective of slowing down climate change enshrined in Art. 20a GG only through international cooperation. It has taken action to this end by ratifying the Paris Agreement, which provides the framework within which it is now also fulfilling its more extensive climate action obligations arising from Art. 20a GG".[59] Interference with the exercise of fundamental rights can be justified only by compliance with Article 20a, and the law must therefore be assessed against

57 The South African High Court, e.g., has indicated that domestic courts have to interpret the law in accordance with international climate treaties because of the obligation to incorporate international law into domestic law. South Africa's High Court, *EarthLife Africa Johannesburg v. Minister of Environmental Affairs and Others, op. cit.*, § 83.

58 "Protection of the natural foundations of life and animals Mindful also of its responsibility towards future generations, the state shall protect the natural foundations of life and animals by legislation and, in accordance with law and justice, by executive and judicial action, all within the framework of the constitutional order". Translation found at <https://www.btg-bestellservice.de/pdf/80201000.pdf>.

59 German Federal Constitutional Court, *Neubauer, et al. v. Germany*, 24 March 2021, § 209.

the provisions of the Paris Agreement.[60] The Paris Administrative Court in the *Affaire du siècle* took a different approach but reached a similar conclusion by deriving France's "general obligation" to combat climate change primarily from several provisions of the UNFCCC and of the Paris Agreement. This basis is sufficient to compel the French state to act, by means of measures adopted at the national level, as provided for by international texts.[61]

Finally, several courts have managed to give indirect effect to international climate obligations through the interpretation of domestic law, achieving a result very close to that of a direct-effect provision. In the famous *Urgenda* case, the Hague District Court gave a "reflex effect" to international obligations because of the presumption of compliance with international law by the state. As a result, these norms are taken into account in the interpretation of domestic law.[62] The French Council of State has also recognised an indirect effect of interpretation of climate treaties clauses, in relation to national and European norms which "have precisely the purpose of implementing them".[63]

These decisions can be explained essentially by the nature of most international climate obligations, the execution of which requires one to refer to a due diligence standard derived precisely from international hard and soft law rules.[64] Most national courts consider, for example, that the obligation periodically to re-evaluate NDCs and domestic law in the light of the latest scientific information available is a due diligence obligation. In doing so, international law is integrated into domestic law in two ways: it limits and defines the extent of the state's discretionary power in the performance of its climate obligations, and it gives concrete expression to the standard of care (or duty of care) expected of the state, including under its constitutional law. Taking

---

60 "[T]he route signposted by Art. 20a GG towards globally effective climate action is largely directed through this Agreement", *ibid.*, § 203.

61 Administrative Court of Paris, *Notre Affaire à Tous and Others v. France*, 3 February 2021, § 21.

62 The Hague District Court, *Urgenda Foundation v. State of the Netherlands*, *op. cit.*, § 4.43: "a state can be supposed to want to meet its international-law obligations. From this it follows that an international-law standard – a statutory provision or an unwritten legal standard – may not be explained or applied in a manner which would mean that the state in question has violated an international-law obligation, unless no other interpretation or application is possible.... This means that when applying and interpreting national-law open standards and concepts, including social proprietary, reasonableness and propriety, the general interest or certain legal principles, the court takes account of such international-law obligations. This way, these obligations have a 'reflex effect' in national law".

63 French Council of State, *Commune de Grande-Synthe v. France*, *op. cit.*, § 12.

64 See *supra*, Chapter 2, 4.3.

the interests of future generations and intergenerational equity into account is also based on international climate law.[65] Many domestic courts insist in particular on the recognition by the state of its capacity to act in the fight against climate change, especially in view of the fact that it has accepted several international commitments.[66]

Facing the global risk of climate change, it is therefore the articulation of hard- and soft-law norms (international as well as national or regional), which allows national courts to give effect to primary international obligations of states.

Currently, as already seen, pandemic domestic litigation is mainly grounded on the breach of human rights treaties which claimants can directly rely on, thus avoiding issues of "integration" of international law into national law. But some plaintiffs who tried to sue China and the WHO before United States courts – which in most cases dismissed their claims on the basis of jurisdictional immunities – also relied on obligations contained in the IHR.[67] If they agreed to examine the merits of these claims against foreign states or international organisations or if they examined it in a lawsuit brought against their own state, domestic courts would be faced with issues similar to those of climate litigation, since the IHR have most probably no direct effect in domestic legal systems. The question remains open whether they would rely on the "reflex effect" or indirect effect doctrine in order to implement obligations contained in the IHR.

4.2 *Contribution to the Effectiveness of Secondary Obligations of States*

In many cases in which national courts uphold the claims of state negligence in relation to global risks, their decision also indirectly constitutes recognition of an internationally wrongful act of that state. Sometimes they explicitly rule on the violation of international legal norms when assessing state responsibility or when reviewing the legality of the state's acts. This breach may be the result of the misbehaviour of executive bodies as well as of legislative bodies. Negligence of Parliaments can, for example, consist in the failure to adopt a climate act or an act on the preparation of the health system for the outbreak

65 See German Federal Constitutional Court, *Neubauer, et al. v. Germany*, *op. cit.*, § 142.

66 Administrative Court of Paris, *Notre Affaire à Tous and Others v. France*, 3 February 2021, § 21.

67 See C.I. Keitner, "To Litigate a Pandemic: Cases in the United States Against China and the Chinese Communist Party and Foreign Sovereign Immunities", *Chinese Journal of International Law*, 2020/2, at 229–236 and <https://www.forbes.com/sites/rachelsandler/2021/04/05/judge-dismisses-lawsuit-against-who-over-its-COVID-19-response/?sh=5cd4ae931a1e>.

of a pandemic. Negligence of governments or other executive bodies can be grounded on the non-implementation of preventative measures against global risks. The Colombian Supreme Court ruled on the breach of international obligations that make up an "ecological public order" consisting, among others, in Colombia's commitments to combat deforestation under the UNFCCC.[68] The Municipal Court of Prague considered that the absence of a Czech reduction plan in accordance with the new NDC of the European Union constituted a breach of the Paris Agreement's obligations.[69]

The Supreme Court of Guatemala has, for example, held that the lack of protection of healthcare workers during the COVID-19 pandemic by the Ministry of Health constituted a violation of the obligations related to their right to health as provided for in Article 11.1(f) of the Convention on the Elimination of All Forms of Discrimination against Women, Article 25 of the International Convention on the Rights of Persons with Disabilities, Article 24 of the Convention on the Rights of the Child, Article 10 of the Protocol of San Salvador and Article 12 of the International Covenant on Economic, Social and Cultural Rights.[70]

In these cases, domestic courts have the opportunity to contribute to the determination of an internationally wrongful act, either when an international right of an individual against a state is at stake or when they have this power by virtue of national law.[71] In the former case, domestic courts sometimes also implement rules of international responsibility triggered by the breach of a primary obligation.

Once an internationally wrongful act has been identified, national courts can also contribute to the implementation of international rules on state responsibility by ruling on its legal consequences. The first measure may be to order the cessation[72] of the wrongful act of negligence in the fight against global risks. This is usually the main "remedy" asked for by claimants in climate litigation. The Colombian Supreme Court, for example, agreed to issue an

---

68 Supreme Court of Colombia, *Future Generations v. Ministry of the Environment and Others*, *op. cit.*, at 22.

69 Prague Municipal Court, *Judgment No. 14A 101/2021*, *op. cit.*, § 280.

70 Guatemala, Constitutional Court, 28 January 2021, Expediente 2758–2020, at 11.

71 A. Nollkaemper, "Internationally Wrongful Acts in Domestic Courts", *AJIL*, 2007, at 760–799.

72 According to article 30 of the ARSIWA, "The State responsible for the internationally wrongful act is under an obligation:
(a) to cease that act, if it is continuing …".

injunction ordering the government to reduce deforestation.[73] The Nepalese Supreme Court also ordered the government to submit and implement a climate law in compliance with Nepal's commitments under the Paris Agreement and specified the conventional provisions this Act should take into account.[74]

Domestic courts may strengthen their rulings by setting specific deadlines for the execution of their orders – and thus the cessation of the internationally wrongful act – by the state. The Municipal Court of Prague, for example, decided that the government would have to take necessary steps to reduce GHG in the fields of energy, transport and forestry within six months.[75] An Appellate Court in Pakistan, which had found that the claimant's human rights had been breached by the government's insufficient action in combating climate change, not only ordered the effective implementation of existing legislation, but decided furthermore to establish a commission in charge of assessing the compliance of the executive with this order.[76]

Turning to pandemic litigation, an Appellate Court of Paraguay, having ruled that the Ministry of Public Health and Social Welfare had been negligent in the protection of the right to health of claimants – as enshrined in several international treaties – ordered it to take all measures necessary for the protection of core aspects of the right to health.[77]

These kinds of orders, which, even if addressed to the executive, may also entail effects for legislative bodies, may thus have several objects: to carry out a climate or health impact assessment, to revise legislation or targets, to adopt more efficient measures. Sometimes national courts may also have the power to cancel or repeal a domestic act incompatible with the state's international commitments. The main consequence of the finding of a violation of international law is thus the non-application of domestic law.[78]

Finally, national courts can contribute to the reparation of damage caused by the failure to address global risks, even if this is not the main purpose of litigation.[79] In the *Affaire du siècle*, the French administrative court agreed to award compensation for the moral damage to the plaintiffs and declared

---

73 Supreme Court of Colombia, *Future Generations v. Ministry of the Environment and Others*, *op. cit.*, at 45.

74 Supreme Court of Nepal, *Shrestha v. Office of the Prime Minister et al.*, *op. cit.*, § 6.

75 Prague Municipal Court, *Judgment No. 14A 101/2021*, *op. cit.*, § 334.

76 Lahore High Court, *Leghari v. Federation of Pakistan*, *op. cit.*, § 8.

77 Paraguay, Civil and Commercial Court of Appeals of Asunción, Fifth Chamber, *Ministry of Public Health and Social Welfare s/Ampa*, 15 June 2021.

78 On this issue see A. Nollkaemper, *National Courts and the International Rule of Law*, Oxford University Press, 2011, at 166.

79 See A. Nollkaemper, *ibid.*

that the ecological damage could also in principle be compensated.[80] At the international as well as at the domestic level, courts are thus starting to consider legal regimes of liability as encompassing interests beyond those of specific subjects. As regards COVID-19 litigation, the claimant before the French Council of State asked for compensation for her physical and moral harms.[81]

5 Towards a Common Regime of Responsibility for Global Risks

The choice of a regime of responsibility (of states and of international organisations) depends on what is at stake and on the priorities in the fight against global risks. The main features of this regime differ according to the aim pursued: to compensate for the harm suffered by victims, to sanction the author of a wrongful act or to avoid possible repetitions of breaches of legal obligations – a deterrent function.

We could deduce from the limits and loopholes of current regimes of responsibility that liability is not the appropriate means of dealing with global risks. However, this conclusion is challenged by two observations. First, a very extensive litigation practice on corporate and state climate liability, on the one hand, and on state responsibility for the COVID-19 pandemic, on the other, is currently developing around the world. Second, doubts about the ability of a liability regime to promote the anticipation necessary to confront this type of risk can be removed if we agree to depart from an overly narrow understanding of the concept of responsibility. Some authors have shown that in Roman law, for example, the notion of *responsor* was originally detached from any fault insofar as it designated only the "guarantor of the course of future events"; following this approach, the term of "responsible" therefore first referred to the equilibrium that was to be guaranteed and not to the subject that had to repair damage.[82] Other legal cultures also include responsibilities that are detached from the notion of fault or wrongful behaviour and are related to the position of the person who must "answer for" something. Herbert Hart refers, for example, to role-responsibility in common law, which derives from the position assumed by a subject from which duties to act with care and diligence in

80 Administrative Court of Paris, *Notre Affaire à Tous and Others v. France*, 3 February 2021, *op. cit.*, §§ 40–42.

81 French Council of State, *Mme M.B.*, 28 June 2022, no 2012679/6-3.

82 M. Villey, "Esquisse historique sur le mot responsable", *Archives de philosophie du droit*, 1977, at 46.

his "sphere of responsibility" arise in the long term.[83] The study of other legal traditions reveals that responsibility can be seen as deriving from the role of humans as guardians of the natural environment and can therefore be conceived in terms of "the burden to be assumed, the conduct to be maintained and the equilibrium to be preserved, and not merely as the duty to answer after the fact for harmful events".[84]

Based on different understandings of the notion of responsibility, some authors have for several years imagined a system of preventive legal responsibility or "anticipation responsibility" that would make it possible to anticipate major risks to the environment.[85] This proposal, which may have seemed rather remote a few years ago, is being translated into the current emergence of climate liability, which could be a source of inspiration for other global risks. Litigation concerning climate liability is developing at both the international and regional levels.[86] But it is above all before domestic courts that hundreds of applications are currently being made to hold states and companies accountable in this respect, on all continents and in relation to both climate and pandemic risks.[87] This litigation, which sees the various courts dealing with very similar legal challenges in terms of liability, ends up creating a convergence of solutions outlining a global liability regime beyond the traditional divisions between branches of law; this constitutes a real turning point.[88] While maintaining great caution in the analysis of distinct legal systems, it becomes possible to benefit from a comparative approach to the case law of the various jurisdictions that have ruled on climate liability. This practice can be grouped around three types of liability litigation, depending on the relationships involved: interstate litigation, litigation initiated by a private or public actor against a state or against an international organisation, and

83 H.L.A. Hart, *Punishment and Responsibility: Essays in the Philosophy of Law*, Oxford, Clarendon Press, 1968, at 212–213.

84 A. Supiot, "Face à l'insoutenable: les ressources du droit de la responsabilité", at 18, in A. Supiot, M. Delmas-Marty (eds), *Prendre la responsabilité au sérieux*, Paris, PUF, 2015, 430 p. My translation.

85 See, taking as a starting point the theory of Hans Jonas, C. Thibierge, "Avenir de la responsabilité, responsabilité de l'avenir", *Recueil Dalloz*, 2004, at 577. See also the idea of "project responsibility" referring to an objective liability for risk created in F. Ost, *La nature hors la loi: l'écologie à l'épreuve du droit*, Paris, La Découverte, 2002, at 296.

86 International litigation, including several requests for advisory opinions, has been mentioned in the introduction. See also, e.g., in the European Union, ECJ, *Armando Ferrão Carvalho and Others v. The European Parliament and the Council*, 25 March 2021.

87 See the two databases mentioned in the Introduction.

88 See M. Torre-Schaub, "Justice climatique: vers quelles responsabilités allons-nous?", *Revue juridique de l'environnement*, 2019, at 129.

litigation between private actors – the last two categories often having a transnational dimension. The following discussion focuses solely on the different types of state responsibility, although it should be borne in mind that common legal issues arise in relation also to the responsibility of companies and of international organisations. But the responsibility of these two kinds of actors is not studied in this section. First, the domestic responsibility of companies cannot provide useful insights into international responsibility issues and, secondly, there is not much practice on international organisations' responsibility before domestic courts because their jurisdiction is barred by immunities.

A new legal regime of "responsibility for global risks" is currently emerging which has similar characteristics in domestic, regional and international law. Its main features concern the criterion triggering state responsibility (5.1), the characteristics of reparable harm (5.2) and the anticipation function (5.3).

5.1 *From the Internationally Wrongful Act to the Link with Global Risks*

Most GHG emissions – the direct causes of climate change – come from private actors, not from states. In a similar vein, several activities at the origin of a pandemic – such as transport, trade, medical activities … – pertain to private actors, while states should take all measures necessary to avoid damage resulting from the spread of a pandemic. States can therefore be held responsible for their inaction with regard to the activities, most often lawful, of actors under their control, i.e. in their sphere of power. It is precisely this control that gives rise to a duty of care in the exercise of the state's preventative power. When several factors can cause, contribute to or avoid the risk of damage, the classical liability regime is not sufficient. There is a need for criteria linking the occurrence of the risk to one or more actors involved. "What matters is not direct causality between action and damage but the proximity of an actor to a risk".[89] Once this link has been established, it is only *a posteriori* that the negligence of the state can be identified, by reference not to the violation of specific obligations – and therefore to a wrongful act – but to a standard of due diligence construed on a case-by-case basis and according to changing circumstances. The main obstacle in the search for state responsibility based on an internationally wrongful act for global risks is that most activities that cause greenhouse gas emissions or that are at the origin of the spread of pathogens are not prohibited, and it is therefore difficult to identify a breach of specific obligations. As mentioned, there are international legal regimes for combating

89 H. Krieger, A. Peters, "Due diligence and structural change in the international legal order", at 379, in H. Krieger, A. Peters, L. Kreuzer (eds), *Due diligence in the international legal order*, Oxford University Press, 2020, XVIII–402 p.

climate change and for preventing the outbreak of epidemics, but the obligations arising therefrom tend to be rather vague and general. The cause (*stricto sensu*) of possible state liability in this case does not really lie in fault or misbehaviour, understood as the violation of a precisely determined obligation, which has led some authors to wonder whether this type of liability can be disconnected from the notion of wrongfulness.[90]

However, if we turn again to the example of Roman law, in the Digest the reparation of damage is based not on fault but on the notion of justice as a just distribution, as a balance (*suum cuique tribuere*), and therefore on the disturbance of that balance, whatever the cause. The consequences of this imbalance must then be distributed among those who are "responsible" for it in the sense of guarantors of the equilibrium. If this reasoning is transposed to cases of shared responsibility in the face of global risks, it can be considered that responsibility should fall on those who have knowledge of the risk and above all who have the power to prevent damage. It is, therefore, the exercise of this power, rather than the implementation of an obligation, that must be carried out diligently.[91] The notion of diligence thus establishes a link between a power of influence and the overall risk, in this case climate change or a pandemic. This power of the state is exercised above all in the area of prevention insofar as these risks are established by the work of experts such as the IPCC and the WHO, but it is also precautionary in certain respects. The notion of diligence is found in various legal systems, such as international and constitutional law as a duty of care, public trust (which allows future generations to be taken into account), etc. However, it is the link between the state and the source of the risk that is the basis of this duty to act diligently, which makes it necessary to identify the criteria for the control it exercises over the actors at the origin of harmful emissions. In international law, the first criterion used is territorial: the state is supposed to prevent harmful acts that emanate from its territory. This has been confirmed quite logically by several domestic courts. For example, the Dutch court used this criterion to consider, in the *Urgenda* case, that the state has the power to control the overall level of emissions in the

90 A. Nollkaemper, "Responsibility", at 764, in J. D'Aspremont, S. Singh (eds), *Concepts for International Law: Contributions to Disciplinary Thought*, Cheltenham, Edward Elgar Publishing, 2019, X–946 p.

91 "The essence of this conceptual shift towards responsibility, however, is that the existence of an international agreement and obligations is no longer the raison d'être of action", A. Macey, "The principle of responsibility in the global response to climate change", at 124, in B. Martin, L. Te Aho, M. Humphries-Kil (eds), *Responsability. Law and governance for living well with the Earth*, New York, Routledge, 2019, XII–266 p.

Netherlands, which it confirmed by ratifying several international treaties.[92] According to the Colombian Supreme Court, domestic authorities should have used their power to control the exploitation of the Amazon Forest in the country's territory by all possible means, including seeking the assistance of local authorities.[93] Several domestic courts have also held that states have the obligation to take all reasonable measures aimed at protecting their populations from the contagion of an epidemic and to institute healthcare services capable of coping with it.[94] The French Council of State also considered that "the risk of the emergence of a respiratory pathogen causing a pandemic was known by the scientific community and by the French health authorities. Furthermore, the state was aware that such masks were one of the main means of protection in the context of such an epidemic, particularly in a phase where neither vaccine nor treatment would be available".[95]

The question remains whether this control can also be taken into consideration extra-territorially, with regard to actors that carry out abroad their main activity to which state legislation is at least partly applicable. In inter-state relations, the International Court of Justice has held that, according to the principle of prevention, "the state is obliged to use all the means at its disposal to prevent activities taking place in its territory, or in any area under its jurisdiction, from causing significant harm to the environment of another state".[96]

More generally, international courts and conventional bodies have held that states may be found responsible when their omissions in the protection of human rights have foreseeable international consequences,[97] including on the basis of due diligence.[98]

5.2 *From Certain to Potential Harm*

One of the main difficulties in recognising liability for global risks lies in causation; because a series of acts and omissions of different actors are at the origin

92 The Hague District Court, *Urgenda Foundation v. State of the Netherlands*, *op. cit.*, 4.66.

93 Supreme Court of Colombia, *Future Generations v. Ministry of the Environment and Others*, *op. cit.*, at 42.

94 See, e.g., Paraguay, Civil and Commercial Court of Appeals of Asunción, Fifth Chamber, *Ministry of Public Health and Social Welfare s/Ampa*, *op. cit.*

95 My translation, § 7.

96 ICJ, *Pulp Mills on the River Uruguay* (*Argentina v. Uruguay*), *op. cit.*, § 101.

97 Human Rights Committee, *Munaf v. Romania*, 21 August 2009, § 14.

98 IACHR, *Velasquez Rodriguez v. Honduras*, 29 July 1988, § 172. See also M.E. Salomon, "How to keep promises: making sense of the duty among multiple States to fulfil socio-economic rights in the World", at 366, in A. Nollkaemper, D. Jacobs (eds), *Distribution of responsibilities in international law*, Cambridge University Press, 2015, XXIV–448 p.

of these risks, it is difficult to determine which causes can be considered as relevant for liability purposes. The United States Supreme Court addressed these issues in the *Massachusetts v.* EPA case concerning the failure of the Environmental Protection Agency (EPA) to regulate GHG emissions, the law stating that the EPA could refuse to regulate pollutant emissions only once it had determined that the pollutants did not contribute to climate change. The EPA questioned the link between its failure to regulate and the damage claimed by the plaintiffs, arguing that its regulation would have been ineffective because it could have produced benefits only in the long term and because it would at best have only slowed climate change in the absence of sufficient action by other states. The Court refuted this argument by recalling first of all that general causality between GHG emissions and climate change was established and, consequently, that the EPA's refusal to act undoubtedly contributed to this phenomenon. Moreover, because of the seriousness of the consequences of climate change, any reduction in these emissions was a necessary contribution, regardless of when the action became effective or of the behaviour of other polluters.[99] The same type of reasoning was used in the *Urgenda* case by the Dutch court, according to which causality is demonstrated by several scientifically established facts: Dutch GHG emissions certainly contribute to climate change at the global level; climate change has already had various effects in the Netherlands; if GHG emissions are not reduced, there is a likely risk of very serious and irreversible damage.[100] Concerning health litigation, the French Council of State considered that France was aware of the pandemic risk and should have taken preventive measures, even if on the other hand "in the exceptional circumstances resulting from the appearance of the virus responsible for COVID-19 and taking into account in particular the modes of transmission of the virus, the objective of protecting public health could not consist of simply preventing the appearance of an epidemic on the national territory".[101]

According to these decisions, it is sufficient to show that the state's inaction contributes to increasing the risk of serious and irreversible damage caused by climate change or by a pandemic in order to establish a causal link. The precautionary principle makes it possible definitively to establish the causal link between the contribution of a state's conduct – even if it took place several

99 United States Supreme Court, *Massachusetts et al. v. Environmental protection agency et al.* (*Massachusetts v.* EPA), *op. cit.*, at 21–23.

100 The Hague District Court, *Urgenda Foundation v. State of the Netherlands*, *op. cit.*, §§ 4.76 à 4.90.

101 § 6, my translation.

years before the occurrence of the risk – and the probable overall harm done. Causality is thus established on a probabilistic basis, relying on the certainty of the contribution of the state's negligence. This reasoning in environmental matters was also adopted by the International Court of Justice in a 2018 judgment.[102] Insofar as its responsibility is based on the control that the state exercises over the risk, that state cannot rely on the shortcomings of other countries to exonerate itself from its responsibility on the ground that it is not in a position to achieve the goal of prevention by itself. This was clearly stated by the Dutch judge in the *Urgenda* case,[103] as well as by the German Federal Constitutional Court. According to the latter, Article 20a of the Basic Law requires the state to seek a solution to the problem of climate change, including at the international level. Germany cannot therefore avoid its responsibility by relying on the GHG emissions of other states.[104] Moreover, by referring to the contribution to global damage, the responsibility of states could be calculated on the basis of the share of GHG emissions from companies under their control over a certain period.[105] André Nollkaemper and Dov Jacobs consider that, in cases of shared responsibility, liability can be distributed by way of several criteria including the content of primary obligations, the nature of the contributions to the damage, the use of causality in relation to reparation and not with regard to liability, and the power of influence on other actors and equity.[106]

When a court questions the responsibility of a state for failure to take due care in preventing climate change caused by actors under its control or to take the measures necessary to prevent the spread of a pathogen, most of this damage has not yet occurred. Moreover, other damage is also the result of past negligence that is not attributable to the state concerned. The damage caused by climate change and by pandemics is necessarily collective in nature and difficult to individualise, as the phenomenon has a global dimension. With regard to climate change, the main victims are the international community – including

102 ICJ, *Certain Activities Carried Out by Nicaragua in the Border Area* (*Costa Rica v. Nicaragua*), Judgment, 2 February 2018, § 34.

103 The Hague District Court, *Urgenda Foundation v. State of the Netherlands*, *op. cit.*, 4.66.

104 German Federal Constitutional Court, *Neubauer, et al. v. Germany*, *op. cit.*, § 199.

105 On the contribution of attribution science to the determination of causality see M. Burger, J. Wentz, R. Horton, "The Law and Science of Climate Change Attribution", *Columbia journal of environmental law*, 2020, at 57. Evidence of a causal nexus between state negligence in restricting GHG emissions and specific harm was extensively discussed in the famous case *Juliana v. United States*, No 18-36082, 9th Cir., 17 January 2020.

106 A. Nollkaemper, D. Jacobs, "Introduction: mapping the normative framework for the distribution of shared responsibility", at 22–30, in A. Nollkaemper, D. Jacobs (eds), *Distribution of responsibilities in international law*, Cambridge University Press, 2015, XXIV–448 p.

future generations – and the environment itself. The question is whether a state can be held liable for damage that is not yet entirely present and what type of damage can be remedied. The precautionary principle can contribute to the identification of reparable damage.[107] This kind of approach can also help one to understand how to use responsibility in order to perform the function of combating global risks: "the Pigovian function of international law is to bring the international effects of national decisions to bear on national authorities, where, as Coase pointed out, it is worthwhile in transaction cost terms to do so".[108] Climate damage is one of the main types of environmental damage, i.e. damage considered solely in relation to the environment, apart from the loss caused to human activities. It is the principal expression of the common concern of humankind in this area. The International Court of Justice recognised the justiciability of ecological damage for the first time in 2018,[109] and many states have also enshrined it in their regulations. This is notably the case in France, which has introduced it into Article 1246 of its Civil Code. Remarkably, administrative courts have also taken into consideration this damage in the context of state responsibility since the decision in the *Affaire du siècle*, specifying that this peculiar harm is likely to occur in the future, even if some of its elements may already have been established. In its second judgment, the Paris Administrative Court insisted on the future nature of ecological damage: "[t]he ecological damage resulting from a surplus of greenhouse gas emissions is continuous and cumulative in nature, since the failure to comply with the first carbon budget has led to additional greenhouse gas emissions, which will be added to the previous ones and will produce effects throughout the life of these gases in the atmosphere, i.e. approximately 100 years".[110] In addition to ecological harm, climate change affects individual and collective rights and the interests of many actors (states, individuals, peoples, etc.).[111] The legal regime of international responsibility allows a non-specifically injured state to claim

107 M.G. Faure, A. Nollkaemper, *op. cit.*, at 43.

108 J.P. Trachtman, "*Ex ante* and *ex post* allocation of international legal responsibility", at 103, in A. Nollkaemper, D. Jacobs (eds), *Distribution of responsibilities in international law*, Cambridge University Press, 2015, XXIV–448 p. The author here draws a parallel with the notion of Pigovian tax. A Pigovian (named after the British economist Arthur C. Pigou) tax is a tax placed on any good which creates negative externalities and the aim of which is to impose an additional cost on actors not directly involved in the transaction in order to create a more socially efficient allocation of resources.

109 ICJ, *Certain Activities Carried Out by Nicaragua in the Border Area (Costa Rica v. Nicaragua)*, Judgment, 2 February 2018, § 41.

110 Administrative Court of Paris, *Notre Affaire à Tous and Others v. France*, 14 October 2021, §11. My translation.

111 See *supra*, Chapter 3, 2.

reparation "in the interest of the beneficiaries of the obligation breached"[112] in the broadest sense. In this perspective, the essential function of responsibility is to compel the state to abide by its duty of care for the future, rather than to repair the effects of the past.

5.3 *From Reparation to Anticipation*

Most of the current liability regimes aim to provide compensation for damage that is identifiable as having occurred in the past. As mentioned above, the very characteristic of the damage produced by global risks is that it is complex and not entirely assessable at a given moment. The aim of all the claimants in bringing liability actions against states is rather to obtain orders that those responsible take effective action to prevent future risk. They thus seek essentially protective effects. Once again, if we consider a broader understanding of liability, we see that the restoration of the broken balance in the perspective of Roman law does not refer only to the reparation of damage. Similarly, any type of liability also has a preventive function alongside that of reparation; the challenge of liability for global risks is that the balance is reversed: the preventive function then takes priority. The role of courts in this litigation is therefore decisive in two respects: on the one hand, they can order the state to act with diligence in the specific case submitted to them, and, on the other hand, they are responsible for giving content, at a given moment, to the standard of diligence to be followed in the future. In this way, courts contribute to the strengthening of the legal regimes of prevention of global risks which often cannot include very accurate obligations because of the uncertainty inherent in these risks. Precaution can thus have a dual function in terms of liability: to form the basis for the prevention of GHG emissions or of actions leading to the spread of a pandemic and to determine the degree of predictability that allows causality to be established with the negligence of states.

To the extent that they incorporate a preventative dimension, some liability regimes already provide for the possibility of ordering forward-looking measures. In international law, for example, the responsible party may be compelled to cease violating its obligations, to provide guarantees of non-repetition of its negligence or even measures of satisfaction by way of reparation, such as the constitution of a fund intended to contribute to the adaptation to climate change of the victim state. In climate and health litigation the plaintiffs always aim primarily to obtain an injunction against the state to adopt the necessary

112 Article 48 of the ARSIWA on the invocation of responsibility by a State other than an injured State.

preventive measures.[113] Regardless of the type of action sought, most courts have the power to act preventatively. Article 1252 of the French Civil Code, for example, recognises the protective dimension of liability for ecological damage: "[i]ndependently of the compensation for ecological damage, the judge, seized of a request to this effect by a person mentioned in Article 1248, may prescribe reasonable measures to prevent or halt the damage".[114] In almost all the COVID-19 cases, domestic courts ordered states to take measures aimed at preventing the further spread of the pandemic or to combat it in order to avoid greater harm for the population.[115] When they grant the claimants' submissions, national courts contribute to the cessation of states' negligence by their decisions or injunctions. These are aimed at a variety of purposes: conducting impact studies on climate change, revising GHG emission limitation targets, adopting more restrictive measures in several sectors such as the fight against deforestation, taking several measures aimed at protecting the population against a pandemic, taking timely measures to avoid the spread of a pandemic, etc. French administrative courts made use of their power of injunction, emphasising its suitability for the very specific characteristics of ecological damage and its priority over a remedy that is not relevant in this kind of situation: "[w]ith regard to the cumulative effect of the damage linked to the persistence of greenhouse gases in the atmosphere and the damage likely to result from it, in the absence of elements making it possible to quantify such damage, and whereas the request for a symbolic payment of one euro to compensate for the ecological damage has already been considered to be unrelated to the extent of the damage, it is appropriate, as has been said, to order the enactment of such measures within a sufficiently short period of time to prevent the worsening of the damage".[116]

Although courts generally leave it to the government to decide on the precise nature of the preventive measures it is compelled to adopt, they often do not hesitate to impose a fairly short deadline for doing so in view of the urgency of the situation. This was the case, for example, with the German Constitutional

113 For a comparative study of the contribution of domestic courts to the prevention of climate damage see M. Hautereau-Boutonnet, E. Truilhé-Marengo (eds), *Le procès environnemental: du procès sur l'environnement au procès pour l'environnement. Rapport final de recherche*, Mission de recherche Droit & justice, 2019, <http://www.gip-recherche-justice.fr/publication/le-proces-environnemental-du-proces-sur-lenvironnement-au-proces-pour-lenvironnement/>.

114 My translation.

115 See for instance Mexico, Sixth District Court of the State of Sinaloa, 10 May 2021, *op. cit.*

116 Administrative Court of Paris, *Notre Affaire à Tous and Others v. France*, 14 October 2021, §13.

Court, which ordered the state to modify its GHG emissions reduction targets by the end of 2022.[117] Health litigation also shows that what is usually asked of courts is to order the state to adopt measures in order to face the pandemic effectively and to protect the population. This was the case, for example, in a decision of a Mexican court which ordered national and decentralised administrative agencies to fulfill their duties in relation to COVID-19 prevention.[118]

In the case of global risks, the overall damage is caused by concurrent responsibilities, which correspond to situations in which several actors contribute to producing the same indivisible harm. Although it is not a question of collective responsibility – each subject remains individually responsible – generally actors who share responsibility interact with each other so that the action or omission of one has effects on the behaviour of the others. As already mentioned, it would thus be logical to seek to distribute responsibility among the various subjects concerned, the fairest solution seeming to be to take into account the capacity to cause harm or the power of influence of each actor with regard to the risk. The criterion of control could thus be decisive for the distribution of the consequences of liability; the degree of effective power of control would determine the share of liability attributed to each actor. In this sense, some authors propose to rely on the concepts of proportional liability or market share liability used in Canada and in the United States according to the degree of risk of each activity.[119] To date, no real joint and several liability regime has been created in relation to global risks. International law is no more advanced on this point than domestic legal regimes, as it only provides for specific rules when several states have contributed to the same internationally wrongful act, which does not correspond to the hypothesis of concurrent liability specific to global risks.[120] Although the idea of a joint and several liability regime seems ideal at first sight, one might ultimately consider that the allocation of liability is not so problematic as this is not the main objective. Rather the main objective is the prevention function which implies the contribution of each actor to a common effort. Most of the time, however, domestic courts do not have to deal with a possible allocation – or reduction – of the consequences of liability, on the one hand because they have jurisdiction only to examine the liability of a single actor and, on the other hand, because they are asked to order the state to behave diligently in preventing the effects of

117 German Federal Constitutional Court, *Neubauer, et al. v. Germany*, *op. cit.*, § 249.

118 Mexico, Sixth District Court of the State of Sinaloa, 10 May 2021, *op. cit.*

119 L. Neyret, "Construire la responsabilité écologique", at 132, in A. Supiot, M. Delmas-Marty (eds), *Prendre la responsabilité au sérieux*, Paris, PUF, 2015, 430 p.

120 See *supra*, Chapter 3, 2.3.

the occurrence of global risks. This is probably the meaning of the Dutch District Court's statement in *Urgenda* that "emission reduction therefore concerns both a joint and individual responsibility of the signatories to the UN Climate Change Convention".[121] In a similar way, the main purpose of states' responsibility in relation to pandemics is to force them to take effective preventive measures such as the implementation of health services capable of dealing with a pandemic, as provided for by their international obligations.

A concept is particularly relevant to cope with the specific nature of global risks in this regard: common but differentiated responsibilities. It developed in the early 1990s in the environmental field to identify different kinds of obligations for states depending on their past and present contribution to a specific environmental problem and on their level of development.[122] It may be found in most multilateral environmental agreements which use it to set different types of obligations for states cooperating in the pursuit of a common goal. In sum, "the concept of common but differentiated responsibilities constitutes a means of translating the concept of intra-generational equity to the inter-State level, and the South-North context in particular, with a view to attaining sustainable development".[123] Articles 3 and 4 of the UNFCCC, for example, include this notion. Among the principles of the Convention, Article 3 states that "1. The Parties should protect the climate system for the benefit of present and future generations of humankind, on the basis of equity and in accordance with their common but differentiated responsibilities and respective capabilities. Accordingly, the developed country Parties should take the lead in combating climate change and the adverse effects thereof". Article 4 specifies the parties' commitments take this specific approach into account and must thus be read accordingly. The principle of common but differentiated responsibilities has several legal consequences, such as the possibility of requiring only developed states to comply with some obligations, such as specific GHG emissions reductions, which was the case with the Kyoto Protocol.[124]

But this concept may also be useful for the purpose of distributing responsibilities for global risks. As long as the main state obligations in this field require the implementation of due diligence standards, the principle of common but differentiated responsibilities contributes to their definition. Breaches of these

121 The Hague District Court, *Urgenda Foundation v. State of the Netherlands*, *op. cit.*, § 4.79.

122 See Principle 12 of the Stockholm Declaration of the United Nations Conference on the Human Environment and Principles 6 and 7 of the Rio Declaration on Environment and Development.

123 E. Hey, "Common but differentiated responsibilities", *MPEPIL*, 2011, § 5.

124 Article 3 and Annex I.

obligations may thus also be evaluated through the same perspective.[125] More generally, taking common but differentiated responsibilities into account may have consequences for the content of state responsibility by helping to determine the different shares of reparation.[126] This reasoning could be used in regard to climate change liability but also for responsibility linked to pandemic risk. The draft of the WHO convention, agreement or other international instrument on pandemic prevention, preparedness and response explicitly refers to the notion of common but differentiated responsibilities, thus transposing it into global health law. This choice confirms the need for a common approach to several global risks. Article 4, which sets out the Guiding principles and rights, indicates: "[c]ommon but differentiated responsibilities and capabilities in pandemic prevention, preparedness, response and recovery of health systems – All States are responsible for the health of their people, including pandemic prevention, preparedness, response and recovery, and previous pandemics have demonstrated that no one is safe until everyone is safe. Given that the health of all peoples is dependent on the fullest cooperation of individuals and States, all Parties are bound by the obligations of the WHO CA+. States that hold more resources relevant to pandemics, including pandemic-related products and manufacturing capacity, should bear, where appropriate, a commensurate degree of differentiated responsibility with regard to global pandemic prevention, preparedness, response and recovery. With the aim of supporting every Party to achieve the highest level of proven and sustained capacity, full consideration and prioritisation are required of the specific needs and special circumstances of developing country Parties, especially those that (i) are particularly vulnerable to adverse effects of pandemics; (ii) do not have adequate capacities to respond to pandemics; and (iii) potentially bear a disproportionately high burden".[127] The different levels of obligations are clearly related to the common need for cooperation, and this criterion could also be used in order to allocate to the different stakeholders part of the responsibility for the damage caused by a pandemic.

---

125 J. Peel, "The practice of shared responsibility in relation to climate change", at 1009, in A. Nollkaemper, I. Plakokefalos, J.N.M. Schechinger, J.K. Kleffner (eds), *The practice of shared responsibility in international law*, Cambridge University Press, 2017, LXXVI–1152 p.; C. Voigt, "Climate change and damages", at 465, in K.R. Gray, R. Tarasofsky, C. Carlarne (eds), *The Oxford handbook of international climate change law*, Oxford University Press, 2016, XXIV–822 p.

126 A. Nollkaemper, I. Plakokefalos, "Conclusions", at 1104, in A. Nollkaemper, I. Plakokefalos, J.N.M. Schechinger, J.K. Kleffner (eds), *The practice of shared responsibility in international law*, Cambridge University Press, 2017, LXXVI–1152 p.

127 § 8.

6 Conclusions

Traditional responsibility regimes which are turned to the past do not meet the challenges created by global risks: they all face similar difficulties pertaining to causation, reparable damage, the function of anticipation … But two paths may show other perspectives more suitable to global risks. First, even if the most common current liability regimes are based on fault/wrongful acts or strict liability, which are not very helpful in coping with global risks, alternative conceptions of responsibility exist in several parts of the world and have existed in the past. Some of them share the rationale of the guarantee of an equilibrium, including between humans and the Earth. Second, it must not be forgotten that responsibility regimes are shaped according to the specific goal pursued and, in this respect, there may be several overarching objectives: reparation for victims of damage, sanctioning of the actor responsible, and the prevention of renewal of the events at the origin of the imbalance and of possible harm. In the past, responsibility regimes have always been built with at least one of these aims in mind. Responsibility for global risks is no exception, and this evolution is perceptible in current litigation, mainly at the domestic level.

The emerging legal regime of state responsibility for climate change – resulting from national, regional and international court decisions – has original features that distinguish it from most current liability regimes, which are mainly centred on reparation and based on fault. It thus certainly responds to the current challenges posed by the consideration of common concerns of humankind – including future generations – in the face of a global risk, but it is also part of a preventative function that has always been attached to the notion of responsibility, considered broadly. State responsibility for climate change is entirely focused on what this actor is responsible for – in this case, a natural balance – because of its position[128] as guarantor, which gives it influence over this equilibrium; in short, because of the power it exercises. The legal regime then shifts its focus from the subject to the object, from the "responsible" in the modern sense to the "*sponsor*" as identified by Roman law. This also explains why this emerging legal regime is likely to transcend the boundaries between legal fields – as is already the case with the rules of climate law – and to constitute a model for other global risk liability regimes. Even if thus far there have been only threats of international litigation on the responsibility for the outbreak and the spread of the COVID-19 pandemic,[129] the emerging

128 "It would no longer be the commitment but the 'position' of the entities that would make them responsible": M.-A. Frison-Roche, *op. cit.*, at 107. My translation.

129 <https://www.ibanet.org/article/D1B023C0-4033-4197-B68D-C11301478271>.

domestic litigation on this issue can be compared to climate case law on these several issues in order better to understand the current evolution of the function of international law.[130]

130 See, on the possible evolutions of the law of state responsibility, M. Paparinskis, "COVID-19 claims and the law of international responsibility", *Journal of international Humanitarian Legal Studies*, 2020, at 311–330 and M. Paparinskis, "The once and future law of State responsibility", *AJIL*, 2020, at 618–626.

CHAPTER 4

Looking Forward, the Paths of Solidarity

1 Introduction

The term "solidarity" refers to "unity or agreement of feeling or action, especially among individuals with a common interest; mutual support within a group".[1] Stemming from the Latin "*solidus*" – meaning dense, robust – it indicates what binds people together in mutual dependence. The way forward in dealing with global risks seems to rely on this principle, as is shown when looking at current case law and at the most recent legal instruments relating to them. Some economic and legal concepts, such as global public goods, have been imagined precisely to point to a solidarity of faith towards common interests seriously threatened, including the climate and public health (4.1). Using this perspective to take into account the interests put in danger by global risks leads to a change in the rationale used in international law to address them: they cannot be protected only by the rationale of exception, but their protection should be included in the different fields of international law in a mutually supportive way (4.2). Solidarity could then be considered as an emerging principle in international law – as is the case for other issues – aimed at guiding the interpretation and implementation of its different rules in this context (4.3).

2 Climate and Health as Global Public Goods

Currently the protection of the climate and of public health is considered by several treaties as a "common interest of humankind", which entails a series of legal consequences (2.2). But several fora are discussing the possibility of giving them the status of "global public goods" in order to set up specific legal regimes of protection (2.3). The notion of global public goods has been developed in order to address a series of features of some public interests which are common to the whole international community, particularly that part of it that is vulnerable to current risks and which can be protected only by the concerted action of all the stakeholders at different levels (2.1).

1 <https://annalsofglobalhealth.org/articles/10.5334/aogh.3035/galley/3068/download/>.

 | DOI:10.1163/9789004538702_006

2.1 *Global Public Goods and International Law*

According to the writings of Paul Samuelson in the 1950s, a pure public good is characterised by non-rivalry – consumption of the good by one individual does not prevent its consumption by another – and non-exclusion – no one can be excluded from consuming this good; an impure public good, on the other hand, has only one of these features.[2]

The notion of common good was originally developed in economics by Elinor Ostrom in the 1990s;[3] these goods are also non-exclusive, but their use by one person can create rivalry with other users.[4] Even if it refers to a specific community and to the idea of property, it may encompass global commons – such as elements of the environment – or knowledge commons. Following Ostrom, there are two main categories of commons: shared resources that are fairly easily governable and normally concern small communities, and those that concern very large numbers and require multi-level governance. "The 'commons' should then refer only to 'open or shared resources, which concern very large numbers, for which rules of access and/or use exist but which have the characteristic of not being administered by a clearly established and identifiable governance structure capable of ensuring compliance with the rules by users'".[5] Common goods are often linked to fundamental human rights with an intergenerational component.

Two problems pertain to these goods: free riding or the "tragedy of the commons", consisting in the interest of members of the community in not using personal resources to protect the good,[6] and the "prisoner's dilemma" referring to the fact that cooperation would produce a better result in order to protect common goods, but participants may prefer an individualistic position, which leads to the "weakest link" problem – the most concerned actors do not cooperate, thus undermining the whole system.[7] Ensuring the efficient production of public goods requires collective action by all stakeholders to compensate for the deficiency of private initiatives and to ensure that all states share the costs

2 P. Samuelson, "The pure theory of public expenditure", *Review of economics and statistics*, 1955, at 387–389.

3 E. Ostrom, *Governing the Commons. The Evolution of Institutions for Collective Action*, Cambridge University Press, 1990, XVIII–280 p.

4 E. Brown Weiss, *op. cit.*, at 110.

5 B. Coriat, "Biens communs (approche économique)", at 99, in M. Cornu, F. Orsi, J. Rochfeld (eds), *Dictionnaire des biens communs*, Paris, PUF, 2017, XXVIII–1240 p.

6 According to some economists, systemic risks are the current manifestation of the tragedy of the commons. See I. Goldin, M. Mariathasan, *op. cit.*, at 31.

7 V. Vadi, "Beyond known worlds: climate change governance by arbitral tribunals?", *op. cit.*, at 1329.

of the benefits they get from their consumption. These sources of inefficiency are even more important in the case of global public goods, the benefits of which are widely dispersed in both space and time. These flaws are manifest, for example, in the context of the protection of climate and of public health against the risks that threaten them.

The term "global public good" was coined in the 1980s "to refer to human and environmental issues that are closely linked to interactions between nations and global actors".[8] They are goods accessible to all states that do not necessarily have an interest in producing them, and include, for example, climate change and public health. Most authors put forward three definitional criteria: the goods concern all countries or at least people well beyond an identifiable group; their effects reach a large part of the world's population; their effects concern future generations.[9] In some areas, a local approach to global public goods could compensate for the shortcomings of the global approach, as in the case of public health, if a relevant community can be identified. In short, a global public good is a good the consumption of which is neither competitive nor exclusive, is accessible to many countries and to a wide spectrum of their population and concerns present and future generations. The main characteristic of global public goods – compared to global commons – is that we need action and specific measures to produce and maintain them; this is the case with a stable and sustainable climate and global public health or the prevention of pandemics.[10] Experts point to three kinds of loopholes of international law in addressing these global public goods: the link between international law and domestic law, participation of all stakeholders beyond states and incentives for all actors to comply with international agreements.[11] "This means that for international law to be an effective instrument in maintaining the integrity of commons and producing global public goods, the conception of public international law will need to expand to encompass relevant domestic laws, to integrate actors beyond States, and to provide incentives other than traditional aid measures".[12]

It must be recognised that at the moment there is no common legal category universally admitted of global public goods or even of common goods;

8 B. Boidin, "Bien public mondial (approche économique)", at 94, in M. Cornu, F. Orsi, J. Rochfeld (eds), *Dictionnaire des biens communs*, Paris, PUF, 2017, XXVIII–1240 p. My translation.

9 I. Kaul, I. Grunberg, M. Stern, *Global public goods: international cooperation in the 21st Century*, Oxford University Press, 1999, at 94–95.

10 E. Brown Weiss, *op. cit.*, at 112.

11 I. Kaul, I. Grunberg, M. Stern, *op. cit.*, at XXV.

12 E. Brown Weiss, *op. cit.*, at 125.

the only common point between their various manifestations is the idea of collective destination, which entails, for instance, regulation of access to the resource or the creation of governance rules.[13] Although there is no international regime of public goods, some concepts reflect the rationale of global public goods: that is the case with *erga omnes* obligations and the notion of common interest of humankind. The UNDP has also largely promoted global public goods[14] which require specific behaviour from states.[15] The protection of public health, for instance, requires the implementation of sovereign powers by states in accordance with their international obligations, but it is also a limit on the exercise of sovereign powers when an individual action is useless – for example when one is facing global challenges. In the field of international law, the qualification of global public good thus depends either on the intrinsic value of the good – this is often the case for human rights – or on the need for collective protection – the example of the atmosphere corresponding to this second category. *Erga omnes* obligations tend to reconcile these two approaches.[16]

2.2 *Climate and Public Health as Common Concerns of Humankind*

According to Resolution 43/53 of the UN General Assembly of 1988 entitled *Protection of the global climate for present and future generations of mankind*, climate change is a "common concern of mankind". The same qualification is used in the UNFCCC[17] and in the preamble to the Paris Agreement,[18] besides several other international instruments in various fields.[19] This notion does not seem to be immediately enforceable, but it is a catalyst for the development of

13 M. Cornu, "Biens communs (approche juridique)", at 101–103, in M. Cornu, F. Orsi, J. Rochfeld (eds), *Dictionnaire des biens communs*, Paris, PUF, 2017, XXVIII–1240 p.

14 See for instance <https://www.undp.org/asia-pacific/publications/enhancing-provision-global-public-goods-ready-more-realism>.

15 F. Francioni, "Sovranità statale e tutela della salute come bene pubblico globale", at 51–66, in L. Pineschi (ed.), *La tutela della salute nel diritto internazionale ed europeo tra interessi globali e interessi particolari*, Napoli, Editoriale scientifica, 2017, 494 p.

16 A. Nollkaemper, "International Adjudication of Global Public Goods: The Intersection of Substance and Procedure", *EJIL*, 2012/3, at 769–791.

17 Preamble.

18 § 11.

19 See N. Oral, "The global commons and common interests: is there common ground?", at 26, in M. Iovane, F.M. Palombino, D. Amoroso, G. Zarra (eds), *The protection of general interests in contemporary international law: a theoretical and empirical enquiry*, Oxford University Press, 2021, XX–416 p.

obligations of care and for the strengthening of responsibility.[20] After much discussion, it has been preferred to the notion of common heritage of mankind, which focuses on ownership and can lead to the establishment of an international governance for a specific good. Moreover, common concern differs from common heritage since it involves the protection of a common interest and not the provision of a regime of exploitation of a resource or a good.[21] Common concern of humankind refers not to the use of resources, but rather to the interest of their conservation which is common.[22] This notion encompasses the protection of commons and the production and preservation of global public goods, as addressed here.

Common concern of humankind nonetheless implies international cooperation by several kinds of actors – including private ones – to address this issue, and this notion is naturally not limited to a specific area, thus also covering, for example, activities taking place entirely on the sovereign territory of states. It produces at least three types of legal effects. First, states which have jurisdiction over activities or goods linked to the common concern have specific international obligations to act for its preservation. Second, it allows other states to question their inaction in relation to this objective. Third, reference to humankind or humanity makes it possible to take into account a wider spatial and temporal dimension, including the concern of future generations. The idea of common concern goes beyond the interests of states and extends to all of humanity, so that states act as guarantors of that humanity.[23] The common features of instruments that include this notion are that they provide for obligations of cooperation for states, including on a financial level, and that they often refer to the principle of common but differentiated responsibilities.[24]

So far, international instruments have used the notion of common concern above all in relation to elements of the environment – the climate, the

---

20 N. Matz, "The Common Interest in International Law: Some Reflections on Its Normative Content", *Zeitschrift für auslandisches öffentliches Recht und Volkerrecht*, 2002, at 17.

21 F. Soltau, "Common concern of Humankind", at 202, in K.R. Gray, R. Tarasofsky, C. Carlarne (eds), The *Oxford handbook of international climate change law*, Oxford University Press, 2016, XXIV–822 p.

22 N. Oral, "The global commons and common interests: is there common ground?", op. cit., at 29.

23 These effects were evident in the reaction of the French President to Brazil's negligence in the defence of the Amazon Forest which was ruined by wildfires in 2019. <https://www.lemonde.fr/international/article/2019/08/22/incendies-en-amazonie-bolsonaro-denonce-une-psychose-environnementale-le-chef-de-l-onu-se-dit-profondement-preoccupe_5501774_3210.html>.

24 N. Oral, "The global commons and common interests: is there common ground?", *op. cit.*, at 33.

atmosphere, biodiversity – but ongoing discussions explore the possibility of extending it to other common interests such as public health. In a report of the *Institut de droit international*, the rapporteur, Shinya Murase, proposed to extend the notion of common concern of humankind to public health in these terms: "The idea can now be extended to the realm of global public health, as the transboundary and global characteristics of the health impacts from communicable diseases are so much similar to environmental damage".[25] The report was meant to provide insights aiming at the drafting of an international instrument – in the form of an agreement or another type of text – on the prevention of and reaction to epidemics: "since epidemics are matters of common concern of humankind, it is necessary for the international community to respond to them on the basis of international solidarity and cooperation".[26] The same stance was taken by the UN General Assembly in its resolution of 2 April 2020 entitled *Global Solidarity to Fight the Coronavirus Disease 2019 (COVID19)*.[27] For the rapporteur, this qualification entails that the protection of all people from epidemics is an obligation *erga omnes* or *erga omnes partes*,[28] and that the breach of their obligations by states in this regard leads to their joint or shared responsibility.[29] So far, the draft of the WHO CA+ has not explicitly referred to this concept, but it nevertheless includes some of its elements. Article 4, for example, in relation to the principle of solidarity, points to "the common interest" constituted by "a fairer, more equitable and better prepared world" regarding pandemics. The qualification of common interest or concern seems to have become possible for global public health because it depends both on a factual basis – now established in relation to pandemics – and on a legitimising process[30] opened by current negotiations of an agreement on pandemic prevention, preparedness and response.

25 Report of the *Institut de droit international* in 2021 on Epidemics and International Law as a proposal in the context of the drafting of an international agreement on pandemics, § 24.

26 *Ibid.*, § 28.

27 A/RES/74/270, § 28.

28 Report of the *Institut de droit international* in 2021 on Epidemics and International Law as a proposal in the context of the drafting of an international agreement on pandemics, § 56.

29 *Ibid.*, § 158.

30 These two defining elements are pointed to by R. Wolfrum, "Identifying Community Interests in International Law: Common Spaces and Beyond", at 21, in E. Benvenisti, G. Nolte (eds), *Community Interests across International Law*, Oxford University Press, 2018, XXVIII–510 p.

2.3 *Possible Consequences of the Turn towards Global Public Goods*

Climate can be considered as a global public good in the economic sense of the term[31] because it is subject to non-rivalry and to non-exclusion. The UN has also placed public health among global public goods[32] and Article 10, § 2, of the Additional Protocol to the American Convention on Human Rights in the area of economic, social and cultural rights states that "the States Parties agree to recognise health as a public good". The universality of a health need would then lead to the idea of public good. But, from a concrete point of view, the notion of public good does not seem to be appropriate for health products such as medicines, insofar as they are susceptible to appropriation and only generics meet the non-exclusion requirement. Moreover, their development requires a very high degree of technicality and know-how, thus excluding the idea of the sharing of the resources. On the other hand, a WHO study shows that it is possible to conceive of the notion of global public goods for health referring to state health policies that improve health status and have positive externalities.[33] The main consequence would be that the right to health should be implemented beyond a mere individual right, thus becoming the means to protect an essential resource (human health) and being subject to a series of public service mechanisms.[34] For instance, the consumption of a health good creates negative externalities that must be compensated for by public authorities – which was the case with COVID-19 vaccination.

More generally, Joseph Stiglitz cites the environment and public health as global public goods. According to him, this notion is the consequence of the internationalisation of economies. "A good can become progressively public if its production becomes deficient or insufficient in relation to an emergency demand and to needs that appear vital for humanity".[35] He mentions the amendment of the TRIPS Agreement as a success of the conception of health as a global public good in a context of global risks linked to epidemics. The creation of public-private partnerships in the field of research and the

31 Ecological stability is a public good according to I. Goldin, M. Mariathasan, *op. cit.*, at 128.

32 L.C. Chen, T.G. Evans, R.A. Cash, "Health as a Global Public Good", at 284–305, in I. Kaul, I. Grunberg, M. Stern, *Global public goods: international cooperation in the 21st Century*, Oxford University Press, 1999, XXXVIII–546 p.

33 S. Negri, *Salute pubblica, sicurezza e diritti umani nel diritto internazionale*, *op. cit.*, at 45.

34 I. Moine-Dupuis, "Droit international économique, droit à la santé et droit aux medicaments", at 295, in C. Titi (ed.), *Droits de l'homme et droit international économique*, Bruxelles, Bruylant, 2019, 370 p.

35 N. Tanti-Hardouin, "La santé, bien public mondial? Le point de vue de l'économiste", at 176, in R. Mehdi, S. Maljean-Dubois (eds), *La société internationale et les grandes pandémies*, Paris, Pedone, 2007, 222 p.

development of drugs necessary to fight some epidemics, such as the Global Fund to Fight AIDS, Tuberculosis and Malaria, is also a consequence of the conception of health as a global public good.

There are several ways of concretising global public goods in international law. One of these tools can be found in the UN Sustainable Development Goals (SDGS). Several of them concern global public goods such as the end of epidemics (goal 3.3[36]) or the fight against climate change (goal 13[37]). The UN has set up indicators to control and evaluate the implementation of the SDGS;[38] their main legal effects are the coordination of the implementation of treaties and other instruments they refer to and the fact that they are a means of interpretation of sustainable development.[39]

Common concerns are community interests identified but not already protected as legal norms.[40] Even if it is still an ongoing development, taking into consideration common interests threatened by global risks as global public goods could be a solution to overcome the tragedy of commons by involving all stakeholders in their protection. This implies more or less formal communication between different stakeholders, as well as interactions that build trust and cooperation at the international, local, national and transnational levels, following what Elinor Ostrom called a "polycentric governance".[41] A similar stance has been taken by lawyers defending multilevel governance: "[t]he less people are self-sufficient in a globally interdependent world, the more they depend on economic, legal and social cooperation for collective supply of transnational PGS like consumer welfare, public health, food security, climate

36 "By 2030, end the epidemics of AIDS, tuberculosis, malaria and neglected tropical diseases and combat hepatitis, water-borne diseases and other communicable diseases".

37 "Take urgent action to combat climate change and its impacts".

38 UNGA resolution 71/313 of 6 July 2017.

39 W. Huck, "The UN sustainable development goals and the governance of global public goods", at 347, in M. Iovane, F.M. Palombino, D. Amoroso, G. Zarra (eds), *The protection of general interests in contemporary international law*, Oxford University Press, 2021, XX–416 p.

40 See S. Besson, "Community Interests in International Law: Whose Interests Are They and How Should We Best Identify Them?", at 38, in E. Benvenisti, G. Nolte (eds), *Community Interests across International Law*, Oxford University Press, 2018, XXVIII–510 p.

41 "Polycentrism is an approach in which several entities are capable of making reciprocal adjustments, through a structured set of rules, to order their relationships with each other, yet each element behaves regardless of the other elements", quoted by K.G. Sisira, N. Govind, M.B. Pillai, "Polycentric approach in climate change mitigation and adaptation programme", at 71, in M.B. Pillai, G. Ganapathy-Doré (eds), *Global commons. Issues, concerns and strategies*, Los Angeles, Sage, 2020, XIV–290 p.

change prevention, democratic peace …".[42] Another possible effect of the qualification of global public goods would be to foster the introduction and development of mechanisms of mutual support.

3 Mutual Supportiveness

Mere coordination meant to avoid conflicts between the fight against global risks and other objectives pursued by different legal regimes does not seem sufficient to respond to the current challenges. The principle of solidarity suggests an alternative approach based on positive interaction: different legal international regimes may not only tolerate each other but also promote the pursuit of their objectives together, by mutualising the efforts (3.1). Mutual supportiveness has started to have some effects on the global risks of climate change and pandemics, but they are still occasional and rather rare (3.2). The first attempts to develop this new approach have nonetheless opened new perspectives that could lead to a remarkable evolution of the mechanisms of international law (3.3).

3.1 *Origins of the Notion of Mutual Supportiveness*

The principle of mutual supportiveness has been mentioned by the ILC in its work on the fragmentation of international law, but only to a very limited extent, as a mechanism to resolve normative conflicts on an *ad hoc* basis.[43] Its origins go back to Agenda 21, which mentioned the objective of making trade and environment "mutually supportive" and the need to encourage macroeconomic policies that combine economic and environmental objectives, including by providing sufficient financial resources to developing countries.[44] It was then introduced into several treaties, as shown, for example, by the preamble

42 E.U. Petersmann, *Multilevel constitutionalism for multilevel governance of public goods: methodology problems in international law*, Oxford, Hart Publishing, 2017, at 42–43.

43 "Mutually consistent interpretations and 'balancing' of multilevel legal regulation of PGs are the 'ultimate rule of law'", ILC report on the fragmentation of international law, §§ 410 and 488.

44 § 2.9. See also the Doha Ministerial Declaration: "31. In order to enhance the mutual supportiveness of trade and environment, we agree to negotiations, without prejudging their outcome, on:

(i) the relationship between existing WTO rules and specific trade obligations set out in multilateral environmental agreements (MEAs). The scope of the negotiations shall be limited to the applicability of such existing WTO rules between the parties to the MEA in question. The negotiations shall be without prejudice to the WTO rights of any Member that is not a party to the MEA in question;

to the 2001 Stockholm Convention on Persistent Organic Pollutants: "[r]ecognising that this Convention and other international agreements in the field of trade and environment are mutually supportive".

It has emerged in the context of the relationship between trade agreements and multilateral environmental agreements but has also been used by arbitral tribunals in the field of foreign investment. In *S.D. Myers v. Canada*, for instance, the arbitral tribunal refers to several environmental treaties and considers that NAFTA must be interpreted in accordance with the principle that the parties have the right to provide for a high level of environmental protection: "environmental protection and economic development can and should be mutually supportive".[45]

But this is also a very narrow interpretation, since this principle may extend beyond mere non-collision or compatibility between legal regimes; on the contrary, it means that one can reinforce the other. In this sense, mutual support incorporates a goal that must be achieved by all possible means, it is based on objective assessment and not in relation to subjective expectations and it does not deal with mere rights and obligations but with the very purpose and object of legal systems.[46] Mutual supportiveness is thus made up of two elements: a functional one which indicates the pursuit of the same objective by the two legal systems (following the rationale of sustainable development) and a relational one which refers to the cross-cutting nature of the two sectors, i.e. which takes into account the fact that they intersect in relation to many activities. It therefore raises no question of hierarchy. This notion indeed excludes the very idea of possible conflicts; it imposes coordination upstream, when states negotiate new agreements, through the principle of integration.[47]

This principle is also found in some recent trade agreements such as in Article 17.12 of CAFTA: "[t]he Parties recognise that multilateral environmental agreements to which they are all party play an important role in protecting the environment globally and domestically and that their respective implementation of these agreements is critical to achieving the environmental objectives

(ii) procedures for the regular exchange of information between the Secretariats of the MEAS and the relevant WTO Committees, as well as the criteria for the granting of observer status

(iii) the reduction or, as appropriate, elimination of tariff and non-tariff barriers to environmental goods and services".

45 *S.D. Myers, Inc. v. Government of Canada*, 13 November 2000, § 220.

46 L. Boisson de Chazournes, M.M. Mbengue, "A Footnote as a Principle: Mutual Supportiveness and its Relevance in an Era of Fragmentation," at 1615–1637, in *Coexistence, cooperation and solidarity: liber amicorum Rüdiger Wolfrum*, Leiden, Nijhoff, 2012, vol. 2.

47 See *supra*, Chapter 2, 3.

of these agreements. The Parties further recognise that this Chapter and the ECA can contribute to realising the goals of those agreements. Accordingly, the Parties shall continue to seek means to enhance the mutual supportiveness of multilateral environmental agreements to which they are all party and trade agreements to which they are all party". But this principle is not limited to environmental law; for example, the UNESCO Convention on the Protection and Promotion of the Diversity of Cultural Expressions also includes it in its article 20.[48]

Some treaty clauses are framed in such a way that they point to more than passive coordination and include active interaction between the different objectives pursued together. Article 4, § 3, of the Nagoya Protocol on Access to Genetic Resources and the Fair and Equitable Sharing of Benefits Arising from their Utilisation to the Convention on Biological Diversity provides, for example: "[t]his Protocol shall be implemented in a mutually supportive manner with other international instruments relevant to this Protocol. Due regard should be paid to useful and relevant ongoing work or practices under such international instruments and relevant international organisations, provided that they are supportive of and do not run counter to the objectives of the Convention and this Protocol". This expression of mutual support – which includes considerations pertaining to health – involves obligations of coordination for the parties before the implementation of this instrument and also for the courts *ex post*, in their function of adjudication.[49] This kind of clause is useful because often the Vienna Convention rules of interpretation are not sufficient to provide mutual supportiveness: Article 31, § 3 (c), in particular, would allow for mutual support only following "relevant rules of international law applicable in the relations between the parties".

Mutual supportiveness thus constitutes a tool for addressing the flaws of the rationale of exception when facing potential conflicts of interests. This idea was perfectly expressed by the WTO Appellate Body: "certain complex public

---

48 "Relationship to other treaties: mutual supportiveness, complementarity and non-subordination

1. Parties recognise that they shall perform in good faith their obligations under this Convention and all other treaties to which they are parties. Accordingly, without subordinating this Convention to any other treaty,
   (a) they shall foster mutual supportiveness between this Convention and the other treaties to which they are parties; and
   (b) when interpreting and applying the other treaties to which they are parties or when entering into other international obligations, Parties shall take into account the relevant provisions of this Convention ...".

49 L. Boisson de Chazournes, M.M. Mbengue, *op. cit.*

health or environmental problems may be tackled only with a comprehensive policy comprising a multiplicity of interacting measures. In the short-term, it may prove difficult to isolate the contribution to public health or environmental objectives of one specific measure from those attributable to the other measures that are part of the same comprehensive policy. Moreover, the results obtained from certain actions – for instance, measures adopted in order to attenuate global warming and climate change, or certain preventive actions to reduce the incidence of diseases that may manifest themselves only after a certain period of time – can only be evaluated with the benefit of time".[50] Once objectives of interest to the international community are identified – for example in the form of global public goods – mutual supportiveness is a means of ensuring interdependence, complementarity and synergy. Some authors believe that a common concern of humankind at least should be at stake in order to trigger this principle.[51] The principle of mutual supportiveness includes a duty to cooperate, even between states which are not parties to certain treaties, at least in order to make their best efforts to avoid conflicts with interests considered worthy of protection in the clauses in which the principle is found.

Following this logic, the adoption of soft-law instruments could be sufficient – at least in the beginning – to depart from a mere logic of exception and in order to introduce climate and health protection goals into a series of existing legal regimes.

3.2 *Current Implementation in the Context of Global Risks*

Some mechanisms of mutual supportiveness are already in place in the context of global risks, and they seem perfectly suited to their specific characteristics. Regarding climate change, an example can be found in the articulation with the law of the sea. As already argued,[52] the objectives of the fight against climate change and of the protection of the marine environment, respectively included in the Paris Agreement and in the UNCLOS, may be pursued in a mutually supportive way, which is useful because some conflicts could potentially arise between them. A measure considered necessary to address climate change issues could have negative effects on some elements of the marine environment, such as biodiversity for example.

50 Appellate Body, *Brazil—Measures Affecting Imports of Retreaded Tyres*, 3 December 2007, WT/DS332/AB/R, § 151.

51 R. Pavoni, "Mutual Supportiveness as a Principle of Interpretation and Law-Making: a Watershed for the "WTO-and-Competing-Regimes" Debate?", *EJIL*, 2010, at 649–679.

52 See *supra*, Chapter 2.2.

In a similar vein, global health law related to the fight against epidemics can be implemented in a mutually supportive perspective with the planned disaster reduction assessments of the Sendai framework,[53] which is the object of the Bangkok principles for the implementation of the health aspects of the Sendai framework for disaster risk reduction of 2016.[54] In the context of epidemics, a specific soft-law instrument must be noted because, by insisting on mutual supportiveness between intellectual property rights and public health issues, it has laid down the path to a historic amendment to the TRIPS agreement. The Declaration on the TRIPS agreement and public health thus states that "1. We recognise the gravity of the public health problems afflicting many developing and least-developed countries, especially those resulting from HIV/AIDS, tuberculosis, malaria and other epidemics. 2. We stress the need for the WTO Agreement on Trade-Related Aspects of Intellectual Property Rights (TRIPS Agreement) to be part of the wider national and international action to address these problems....

4. We agree that the TRIPS Agreement does not and should not prevent members from taking measures to protect public health. Accordingly, while reiterating our commitment to the TRIPS Agreement, we affirm that the Agreement can and should be interpreted and implemented in a manner supportive of WTO members' right to protect public health and, in particular, to promote access to medicines for all".

Some legal regimes are currently shifting from the mere rationale of exception to an approach mutually supportive of several common concerns, including the fight against climate change and pandemics. This is the case with foreign investment law; specific kinds of foreign investments may indeed contribute to the action against global risks.[55] A first way of dealing with conflicts between international investment rules and these public concerns can be, on the model of the Doha declaration, to adopt interpretative guidelines *ex post*. But this approach seems to be too restrictive efficiently to address the issue in all cases; thus some proposals have emerged for integrating a mutually supportive approach *ex ante* into model clauses used for BITs. An example can be found in the Model International Agreement on Investment for Sustainable

53 G. Bartolini, "Le misure di preparazione alle pandemie previste nei regolamenti sanitari internazionali e la loro (mancata) attuazione », *Comunità internazionale*, 2020/3, at 367–390.

54 See also UNGA resolution 74/218 of 23 January 2020.

55 P. Acconci, "The integration of non-investment concerns as an opportunity for the modernisation of international investment law: is a multilateral approach desirable?", in G. Sacerdoti, P. Acconci, M. Valenti, A.P. De Luca (eds), *General interests of host states in international investment law*, Cambridge University Press, 2014, XVI–462 p.

Development of 2005 drafted by the International Institute for Sustainable Development.[56] It would create the basis for future multilateral and bilateral negotiations to promote investments favourable to the fight against global risks. The Pan-African Investment Code adopted in 2016 – which to date is still a soft-law instrument – provides several legal means of ensuring mutual supportiveness between the objectives of fostering foreign investment and fighting climate change: they include shared obligations between the host state and the foreign investor in terms of technology transfer and the possibility for states to assign performance requirements to investments in some sectors. The reform of International Investment Agreements initiated in 2015 by the United Nations Conference on Trade and Development (UNCTAD)[57] also tries to build on this new approach, which could constitute a model applicable also in other fields relevant to global risks.

3.3 *Future Perspectives of the Role of Mutual Supportiveness in Relation to Global Risks*

Several proposals advise developing the implementation of mutual supportiveness even in the absence of specific clauses, as long as a common concern of humankind can be identified. This is notably the case in relation to climate change and to pandemics. A United States ministerial proposal to the WTO on 17 December 2020 concerned the possibility of considering low environmental standards in some countries as countervailable subsidies in order to try to foster a strengthening of domestic regulation in this field. Even if its implementation may be hindered by several obstacles – such as the need to determine what is a reasonable or an acceptable environmental standard[58] – the same idea could be developed in relation to climate change national legislation and the promotion of "climate-friendly" products. Another way of implementing this approach is to include in international economic agreements non-regression clauses on the protection of common concerns, which mirror the principle of

56 "Article 34 – Relation to other international agreements
(A) The Parties agree that the provisions of other international trade agreements to which they are a Party are consistent with the provisions of this Agreement. The Parties shall seek to interpret such agreements in a mutually supportive manner.
(B) In the event of any dispute arising on this issue, the Parties shall seek to resolve such dispute within the mechanisms of this agreement as a first step.
(C) The Parties hereby re-affirm their obligations under international environmental and human rights agreements to which they are a Party".

57 <https://unctad.org/system/files/official-document/diaepcbinf2020d8_en.pdf>.

58 E. Cima, M.M. Mbengue, "'Kind of Green'. The U.S. Proposal to Advance Sustainability through Trade Rules and the Future of the WTO", *ESIL Reflections*, 2021.

non-regression as enshrined in international environmental law or in human rights law. This principle, which has already been introduced into some international investment agreements,[59] could be generalised in economic treaties because it is an alternative to taking such external interests into consideration as mere exceptions to the legal regimes at issue. Sandrine Maljean-Dubois, for instance, underscores the need to "defragment" the climate legal regime by developing mutual supportiveness with rules pertaining to other branches of international law, such as trade law, investment law, the law of the sea, human rights law … Several normative and institutional means could be used for that purpose, including the development of common standards, public-private partnerships and institutional cooperation.[60]

Mutual supportiveness seems to be at the centre of current evolutions also in relation to public health issues. In particular, the draft of the WHO convention, agreement or other international instrument on pandemic prevention, preparedness and response grounds its defence of the One Health approach on this principle. Article 18 aims at promoting mutual supportiveness by stating, for instance, that "[t]he Parties commit to strengthen synergies with other existing relevant instruments that address the drivers of pandemics, such as climate change, biodiversity loss, ecosystem degradation and increased risks at the human-animal-environment interface due to human activities". More generally, WHO law cannot be considered as self-sufficient and should thus be open to the implementation of mutual supportiveness. The territorial scope of human rights obligations in an epidemic context has, for example, already been extended, in particular in the advisory opinion of the Inter-American Court of Human Rights of 2017[61] and in the statement of the Committee on Economic, Social and Cultural Rights on the COVID pandemic and economic, social and cultural rights of 2020.[62] Moreover, the obligation to prevent, reduce and control disease outbreaks which could be the origin of epidemics is already found also in several maritime and civil aviation law agreements,[63]

---

59 See the example of the Pan African Investment Code.

60 S. Maljean-Dubois, "Quel droit international face au changement climatique?", *Recueil Dalloz*, 2015, at 2263.

61 Interamerican Court of Human Rights, *A Request for an Advisory Opinion from the Inter-American Court of Human Rights Concerning the Interpretation of Article 1(1), 4(1) and 5(1) of the American Convention on Human Rights*), *op. cit.*, § 94.

62 CESCR, *Statement on the COVID-19 Pandemic and Economic, Social and Cultural Rights*, 17 April 2020, E/C.12/2020/1.

63 See S. Murase, "Interrelationship among relevant rules of international law on epidemics", at 35, in S. Murase, S. Zhou (eds), *Epidemics and international law*, Leiden, Brill Nijhoff, 2021, XXXII–708 p.

such as in Article 14 and in Annex 9 standard 8.16 of the Chicago Convention on International Civil Aviation,[64] in the International Convention on Ballast Control and Management[65] or in several guidelines and standards of the Maritime Labour Convention. The implementation of Article 20 of the IHR could thus be reinforced and considered as mutually supportive with the objectives of these treaties.

4 The Emerging Principle of Solidarity and Global Risks

Solidarity appears as an emerging structural principle of international law likely to create both negative and positive obligations aiming at protecting common goods, in particular in the context of global risks. This notion is starting to be used in relation to the prevention of and to the reaction to global risks (4.1). It is thus possible to foresee the main legal effects it could produce in the future in this context (4.2).

64 "Prevention of spread of disease Each contracting State agrees to take effective measures to prevent the spread by means of air navigation of cholera, typhus (epidemic), smallpox, yellow fever, plague, and such other communicable diseases as the contracting States shall from time to time decide to designate, and to that end contracting States will keep in close consultation with the agencies concerned with international regulations relating to sanitary measurer, applicable to aircraft. Such consultation shall be without prejudice to the application of any existing international convention on this subject to which the contracting States may be parties".

65 "Regulation C-2 Warnings Concerning Ballast Water Uptake in Certain Areas and Related Flag State Measures

1. A Party shall endeavour to notify mariners of areas under their jurisdiction where ships should not uptake Ballast Water due to known conditions. The Party shall include in such notices the precise coordinates of the area or areas, and, where possible, the location of any alternative area or areas for the uptake of Ballast Water. Warnings may be issued for areas:
2. known to contain outbreaks, infestations, or populations of Harmful Aquatic Organisms and Pathogens (e.g., toxic algal blooms) which are likely to be of relevance to Ballast Water uptake or discharge;
3. near sewage outfalls; or
4. where tidal flushing is poor or times during which a tidal stream is known to be more turbid....".

4.1 *References to Solidarity in Relation to Global Risks*

In the legal field, the principle of solidarity refers to a "relation between persons belonging to a community of interests, entailing for some the moral obligation not to harm the others and to assist them".[66]

This notion can be rooted in the Roman law concept of *obligatio in solidum*, which started to be used in the 18th Century to refer to the idea of the interdependence of members of an identified and legitimate group.[67] It is mentioned in several treaties belonging to different fields of international law, and notably in relation to the protection of the environment and health. Article 3 (b) of the United Nations convention to combat desertification, for example, provides that "the Parties should, in a spirit of international solidarity and partnership, improve cooperation and coordination at subregional, regional and international levels, and better focus financial, human, organisational and technical resources where they are needed".

References to the solidarity principle may also be implicit, as is the case with the preamble to the WHO Constitution, according to which "[t]he health of all peoples is fundamental to the attainment of peace and security and is dependent upon the fullest co-operation of individuals and States.

The achievement of any State in the promotion and protection of health is of value to all.

Unequal development in different countries in the promotion of health and control of disease, especially communicable disease, is a common danger".

As regards climate change, several domestic courts have underscored the fact that international action is based on the principle of solidarity both between states and with future generations.[68] Solidarity seems thus to be characterised by some specific elements in international law: a reference to common concerns of the international community, the need for specific forms of assistance provided by some actors to others without expectations of reciprocity, a clear identification of those providing it and of its beneficiaries.[69] When pursuing the common defence against global risks, the objectives are also in the interest of those who have to act in solidarity, but these benefits are often perceptible only in the long term. Hans Jonas refers to an idea of solidarity of

66 D. Campanelli, "Solidarity, principle of", *MPEPIL*, 2011.

67 H.P. Hestermeyer, "Reality or Aspiration? – Solidarity in International Environmental and World Trade Law" at 45–63, in *Coexistence, cooperation and solidarity: liber amicorum Rüdiger Wolfrum*, Leiden, Nijhoff, 2012, vol. 2.

68 Supreme Court of Colombia, *Future Generations v. Ministry of the Environment and Others*, *op. cit.*, at 20.

69 *Ibid.*

fate between Man and Nature which entails the obligation for Man to preserve nature for itself.[70]

Solidarity functions as both a catalyst of international obligations and a guiding principle when included in a specific instrument. It focuses on interdependent and joint obligations more than on rights and on the collective dimension of these obligations, as was noted by a Mexican court dealing with climate litigation.[71]

4.2 *Effects of Solidarity in the Fight against Global Risks*

This approach has specific legal consequences for the beneficiaries of solidarity, for those who should provide it because they are in a position of guarantors and, finally, for the global public goods which are the object of the protection. On the beneficiaries' side, the collective dimension encompasses the community beyond individuals, and especially future generations which are threatened by global risks such as climate change or the world population threatened by pandemics with the idea of intergenerational equity. In the context of climate litigation, the Supreme Court of Colombia considered that the environmental rights of future generations are based on the principle of solidarity. It is intrinsically related to the protection of climate because, without action to protect it, the future of humankind may be compromised.[72] The right to a healthy environment, for example, creates community rights beyond individual ones; it may also be realised only by several kinds of actors, beyond states.

As concerns those who are meant to act in solidarity, the principle points to common but differentiated responsibilities of different kinds of actors, including both private and public subjects. This notion is a way to implement intergenerational solidarity at the state level.[73] The Sendai framework for disaster risk reduction 2015–2030, for example, takes up the spirit of the ILC's work in its guiding principles, among which is the obligation for states to cooperate at all levels to reduce risks, in realisation of the solidarity principle. It also implies

70 H. Jonas, *op. cit.*, at 136-138.

71 A Mexican court quotes a judgment according to which the right to a healthy environment "is founded on the idea of solidarity that entails an analysis of legitimate interest and not of subjective rights and freedoms, even, in this context, the idea of obligation prevails over that of right, as we are dealing with collective responsibilities rather than individual prerogatives", Mexico, Eleventh Collegiate Court of the First Circuit in Administrative Matters, *Greenpeace v. Instituto Nacional de Ecología y Cambio Climático and Others, op. cit.*, at 49.

72 Supreme Court of Colombia, *Future Generations v. Ministry of the Environment and Others, op. cit.*, at 20.

73 E. Hey, "Common but differentiated responsibilities", *MPEPIL*, 2011.

accepting external assistance when a state is faced with a disaster:[74] "the international law of disaster relief reflects the concept of solidarity through its emphasis on combined efforts to solve a problem that is bigger than the capacity of any one State (negative solidarity). Moreover, it appears to create an inter-related set of duties to this end, with various and differing responsibilities lying with the affected State, the neighbouring States, other assisting States, intergovernmental organisations, and non-governmental organisations (positive solidarity)".[75] The Supreme Court of Colombia insisted on this concept of individual action as part of a collective responsibility: "[t]he principle of solidarity, for the specific case, is determined by the duty and co-responsibility of the Colombian state to stop the causes of the GHG emissions from the abrupt forest reduction in the Amazon; thus, it is imperative to adopt immediate mitigation measures, and to protect the right to environmental welfare, both of the plaintiffs, and to the other people who inhabit and share the Amazonian territory, not only nationals, but foreigners, together with all inhabitants of the globe, including ecosystems and living beings".[76]

Finally, for the global public goods at stake, solidarity means a turn to responsibility conceived not as retribution based on a wrongful act, but as specific actions required by those who act as guarantors of a common balance, which reminds one of the Roman definition of responsibility.[77] In the event of the occurrence of damage to the global public goods at stake, a regime of joint and several liability would also correspond to the implementation of a solidary approach.

A concrete example of achievement following the principle of solidarity in the context of global risks is considered in the WHO draft of pandemic agreement. Article 4, § 5, on guiding principles and rights indeed focuses on solidarity: "[t]he effective prevention of, preparedness for and response to pandemics requires national, international, multilateral, bilateral and multisectoral collaboration, coordination and cooperation, through global unity, to achieve the common interest of a fairer, more equitable and better prepared world". The draft is entirely based on global solidarity, which is mentioned several times

74 E. Valencia-Ospina, "The work of the International Law Commission on "The protection of persons in the event of disasters"", at 5, in G. Bartolini, D. Cubie, M. Hesselman, J. Peel (eds), *Yearbook of international disaster law*, 2018, Brill Nijhoff, 2020, VIII–516 p.

75 A.G. Koroma, "Solidarity: Evidence of an Emerging International Legal Principle", at 125, in *Coexistence, cooperation and solidarity: liber amicorum Rüdiger Wolfrum*, Leiden, Nijhoff, 2012, vol. 2.

76 Supreme Court of Colombia, *Future Generations v. Ministry of the Environment and Others*, *op. cit.*, § 11.3.

77 See *supra*, Chapter 3, 5.

in its text. Beyond this general approach which permeates the whole of the draft, it underlines the specific need for solidarity with a country which notifies a public health emergency. A concrete result of action based on solidarity is the proposal to establish a WHO Global Pandemic Supply Chain and Logistics Network in order to avoid competition for the supply of medical devices and assets during a pandemic and in order to foster the equitable distribution of these goods. In actions concerning both global risks, solidarity is also conceived as encompassing the interests of future generations.[78]

5 Conclusions

The emerging principle of solidarity appears to be the guiding principle which constitutes the framework of action, while the preservation of the global public goods of climate and health against global risks is the objective, and mutual supportiveness between legal regimes and between global actors is one of the main means of achieving it. Even if this approach is only beginning to be used to meet the challenges of global risks, it marks a change of paradigm from a rationale of fragmentation and exception to recognition of the necessity of taking a holistic stance. This is perceptible in the practice of domestic courts facing litigation on these risks, as well as in recent international practice. This "solidarity shift" could also be useful to address other kinds of global risks where it is already discussed, at least in regional or sectoral initiatives. This is, for example, the case as regards financial risks[79] or cyber-risks.[80]

78 The taking into account of risks of human action for future generations is not totally new in international law. On 8 July 1996, the International Court of Justice handed down its Advisory Opinion on *The Legality of the Threat or Use of Nuclear Weapons*, which responded to the United Nations General Assembly request of December 1994. In its Opinion, the Court explicitly referred to the interests of future generations: "it is imperative for the Court to take account of the unique characteristics of nuclear weapons, and in particular their destructive capacity, their capacity to cause untold human suffering, and their ability to cause damage to generations to come", *op. cit.*, § 36.

79 See for instance J. Tirole, "Country Solidarity in Sovereign Crises", *The American Economic Review*, 2015, at 2333–2363.

80 See for instance, within the European Union, the EU Cyber Solidarity Act proposed by the European Commission on 18 April 2023, with the objective of improving "the preparedness, detection and response to cybersecurity incidents across the EU", <https://digital-strategy.ec.europa.eu/en/library/proposed-regulation-cyber-solidarity-act>.

General Conclusion

The term "responsibility" is more and more often used by lawyers in a broad meaning to replace the notion of legal obligation. This is the case, for example, in international law with the concepts of responsibility to protect or common but differentiated responsibilities. Legally speaking, it is not possible to confuse them or to use them interchangeably. But an accurate analysis of global risks may help to explain this evolution in the vocabulary of international law. These kinds of risks in the fields of the environment, technology, security, economics and society are new not because of their nature but because of their reach and of their level of danger. Their disruptive potential is linked to the fact that, for the first time in history, humanity has the power to threaten the possibility of living on the Earth and its own existence. In the past, legal systems already had to adapt to great challenges and to new types of risks, as was the case after the Industrial Revolution: insurance mechanisms and regimes of strict liability were created precisely in order to face grave risks created by activities considered mostly as beneficial for society. Since the end of the 20th Century, we have been facing a new turning point and lawyers have to meet the challenge to address existential risks that are common to all the international community in a situation characterised by "organised irresponsibility". Indeed, this situation presents a disjunction between power and responsibility: each legal regime by itself is unable to allocate responsibility to the actors at the origin of global risks. Interdependence and retroactions between actions and omissions of different kinds of actors, often in a transnational context, are too complex to be addressed by international law, regional legal regimes or domestic systems alone.

This disjunction between power and responsibility is remarkable in international law, its main weakness being that this legal discipline still places the burden mainly on states, even when they are not the first actors concerned. The challenges of global risks for international law are striking. These risks affect the whole of the international community at the same time, but not with the same intensity. Pandemic rebounds or extreme weather events can hit only some parts of the world's population, while the overall risks exist for everyone. Moreover, international inequalities are much aggravated by global risks: some states are more vulnerable to their effects or do not have sufficiently strong means to respond or adapt to them. We can think, for example, of small developing island states confronted with sea-level rise or of many developing countries unable to buy or to produce the COVID-19 vaccine for their populations. Deterritorialisation is one of the consequences of these risks; being conceived

 | DOI:10.1163/9789004538702_007

as the "detachment of regulatory authority from a specific territory",[1] it undermines the territorial conception of law which forms the traditional basis of the relationship between international and national law. Confronted with phenomena of common interest such as transnational activities, international law tends either to define substantive norms or to distribute jurisdiction among states parties to the treaties concerned in order to regulate them. But these approaches are not efficient in the fight against global risks because states are not the only actors involved and because they are unable to grasp the various interconnections at the origin of global risks. The determination of new relationships between legal systems is then required.

The legal definition of global risks here proposed is a starting point in order to identify precisely the legal challenges created by this phenomenon and to understand the ongoing legal evolutions. These risks are created by multiple causes consisting often in lawful activities and including actions and omissions of different kinds of actors of potentially global reach; they affect common concerns of humankind by producing an overall harm resulting from the accumulation in time and space of many incidents of damage affecting various legally protected interests. First, this definition reveals the core legal issue related to global risks: the need to identify the links between their causes and the guarantors – the "*responsores*" in the Roman-law meaning – of the equilibrium that is threatened by them. This definition also offers the opportunity to analyse global risks beyond their several specific categories.

The practice studied in this book is nonetheless based on two examples: climate change and pandemics. It has shown that a number of developments are underway in international law. The first one consists in the introduction of a new rationale based on mainstreaming global risks concerns into all the decision processes of the different stakeholders – states, international organisations, companies. We have insisted here on states' public policies because at present international law still focuses mainly on them. This integration rationale is also implemented through due diligence obligations and standards, which are a means of insisting on the role of states as guarantors in the face of global risks – even if we mentioned the possibility of turning to this function as regards international organisations too. These evolutions lead to

1 C. Bröhlmann, "Deterritorialisation in International Law: Moving Away from the Divide Between National and International Law", at 86, in J. Nijman, A. Nollkaemper (eds), *New Perspectives on the Divide between National and International Law*, Oxford University Press, 2007, XX–380 p.

a general movement or proceduralisation[2] of international law in its function and in its relationship with other legal regimes. In so doing, international law tends also to be more open to an interdisciplinary understanding of these risks, by creating expert bodies which are charged with working on their continuous objectivation.

The function of international law tends thus to shift to the determination of the operational conditions of the guarantee of the equilibrium and the way the actors who are in a position of guarantors promote action. International law identifies them, sets the main goals and the processes of integration and coordination. Quite paradoxically, it thus becomes much more tied to domestic legal systems than by setting substantial norms of harmonisation.[3] The relative consensus on this role is proven by the fact that the fight against global risks may lead to multilateral initiatives in a period not favourable at all to them: this is the case with the negotiation of the WHO convention, agreement or other international instrument on pandemic prevention, preparedness and response. Domestic climate and health litigation has shown how international law is integrated in new ways – for instance by setting standards of care, even in soft-law instruments – and, conversely, how national law may be at the origin of an emerging common regime of responsibility for global risks that could retroact on international responsibility. By turning to proceduralisation, international law may also perhaps indirectly gain influence over non-state actors.

Moreover, another conclusion points to the fact that other jurisdictional criteria emerge besides territory. The elaboration and implementation of legal norms related to global risks also rest on the criteria of community including all the stakeholders concerned by a specific risk and of temporality which, for example, takes into account the need to prevent future harm or to address events occurring simultaneously in different places.[4] In this regard, Cedric Ryngaert defines the current phenomenon of "re-territorialisation" as "the redefinition of territory as a site for legal-political struggles which are informed by community, temporality, or justice-based arguments, and which

2 On this evolution see H. Krieger, A. Peters, "Due diligence and structural change in the international legal order", at 382, in H. Krieger, A. Peters, L. Kreuzer (eds), *Due diligence in the international legal order*, Oxford University Press, 2020, XVIII–402 p.

3 Evelyne Lagrange formulates the hypothesis of the dominant contemporary function of international law, consisting in "organising relations between individuals and a plurality of political entities with which they come into contact", "L'efficacité des normes internationales concernant la situation des personnes privées dans les ordres juridiques internes", *op. cit.*, at 258. We translate.

4 See C. Ryngaert, "Territory in the Law of Jurisdiction: Imagining Alternatives", *Netherlands Yearbook of International Law*, 2017, at 60–62.

are *multi-scalar*, i.e., not limiting themselves to the scale of the national, but extending to the regional and global".[5] This development is reflected, for example, in measures such as carbon-related border-adjustment taxes or in pandemic preparedness actions. Thus, territoriality is adjusted in order to become a tool contributing also to the protection of global public goods and it "may be explored to fulfill global objectives that are not spatially delimited".[6]

This leads to the legal perspectives opened for the future. We should obviously be cautious not to be over-confident about the prospects opened by some first hints of solidarity in the fight against global risks. The COVID-19 pandemic has shown that, when facing a serious emergency, the first reaction of a majority of states is to close borders and to take individual and uncoordinated action. Caution is thus necessary because we are experiencing a transitional period that will be decisive in the next few years for the future of international law and, possibly, for the future of humanity. The current practice nonetheless shows that some possibilities are emerging of taking non-state actors concerned by global risks into account. Further development of due diligence state obligations to control private actors or of member states' subsidiary responsibility for the negligence of international organisations is not a definitive solution since it tends to interfere with the role of guarantor of some crucial subjects. Some recent practice has shown that other paths could be opened through international law in the near future. The specific function of the WHO, for example, is taken into account in the WHO CA+, and this could lead to the development of role responsibility in the context of pandemic prevention and reaction. Domestic litigation against private companies – mainly multinational ones – also shows that some courts have managed to use the method of indirect effect in order to compel them to respect a duty of care based on the due diligence standard derived from the Paris Agreement, thus ordering them to reduce their GHG emissions.[7] This solution is remarkable because in this case companies have no conventional obligations since they are not parties to international climate agreements. Indirect interpretation and due diligence in regard to the other entities of their group are thus used in a fashion similar to the solution adopted for states.

Further studies on international law and global risks could focus on perspectives not followed here concerning both the comparison of climate change and pandemics with other global risks and the analysis of the methods of mainstreaming used both internationally and at the national level.

---

5 *Ibid.*, at 66–67.

6 *Ibid.*, at 72.

7 See The Hague District Court, *Milieudefensie et al. v. Royal Dutch Shell plc.*, 26 May 2021.

Bibliography

Abate (Randall S.) (ed.), *Climate change impacts on ocean and coastal law: US and international perspectives*, Oxford University Press, 2015.

Acconci (Pia), *Tutela della salute e diritto internazionale*, Padova, CEDAM, 2011.

Acconci (Pia), "The integration of non-investment concerns as an opportunity for the modernisation of international investment law: is a multilateral approach desirable?", in Sacerdoti (Giorgio), Acconci (Pia), Valenti (Mara), De Luca (Anna Pia) (eds), *General interests of host states in international investment law*, Cambridge University Press, 2014.

Alogna (Ivano), Bakker (Christine), Gauci (Jean-Pierre) (eds), *Climate change litigation: global perspectives*, Leiden, Brill Nijhoff, 2021.

Amoroso (Daniele), Iovane (Massimo), Palombino (Fulvio Maria), Zarra (Giovanni) (eds), *The protection of general interests in contemporary international law*, Oxford University Press, 2021.

Arato (Julian), Claussen (Kathleen), Heath (J. Benton), "The Perils of Pandemic Exceptionalism", *AJIL*, 2020, at 627.

Barritt (Emily), Fisher (Elizabeth), Scotford (Eloise), "The Legally Disruptive Nature of Climate Change", *The Modern Law Review*, 2017, at 173.

Bartolini (Giulio), Cubie (Dug), Hesselman (Marlies), Peel (Jaqueline) (eds), *Yearbook of international disaster law*, 2018.

Bartolini (Giulio), "Le misure di preparazione alle pandemie previste nei regolamenti sanitari internazionali e la loro (mancata) attuazione », *Comunità internazionale*, 2020, at 367.

Beck (Ulrich), *Risk society. Towards a new modernity*, London, SAGE Publications, 1992.

Besson (Samantha), "La *due diligence* en droit international", *Collected courses of The Hague Academy of International Law*, vol. 409, 2019.

Bodansky (Daniel), "The legal character of the Paris Agreement", *RECIEL*, 2016/2, at 142.

Bodansky (Daniel), Brunnée (Jutta), Rajamani (Lavanya), *International climate change law*, Oxford University Press, 2017.

Boisson de Chazournes (Laurence), Mbengue (Makane Moïse), "A Footnote as a Principle: Mutual Supportiveness and its Relevance in an Era of Fragmentation", at 1615, in *Coexistence, Cooperation and Solidarity* (2 vols.) *Liber Amicorum Rüdiger Wolfrum*, Leiden, Brill, 2012.

Bourdelais (Patrice), Vagneron (Frédéric), "Understandings of disease transmission in the Western World", in Delaurenti (Béatrice), Le Roux (Thomas) (eds), *Cultures of contagion*, MIT Press, Cambridge, London, 2021, at 165.

Bourg (Dominique), Joly (Pierre-Benoît), Kaufmann (Alain) (eds), *Du risque à la menace: penser la catastrophe*, Paris, PUF, 2013.

Brown Weiss (Edith), "Establishing norms in a kaleidoscopic world", *Collected Courses of the Hague Academy of International Law*, vol. 396, 2019.

Brunnée (Jutta), "The Global Climate Regime: Wither Common Concern?", at 721, in *Coexistence, Cooperation and Solidarity* (2 *vols.*) *Liber Amicorum Rüdiger Wolfrum*, Leiden, Brill, 2012.

Brunnée (Jutta), "Procedure and substance in international environmental law", *Collected Courses of The Hague Academy of International Law*, vol. 405, 2020.

Burci (Gian Luca), Toebes (Brigit) (eds), *Research handbook on global health law*, Cheltenham, Edward Elgar Publishing, 2018.

Burci (Gian Luca), "The Legal Response to Pandemics", *Journal of International Humanitarian Legal Studies*, 2020, at 8.

Burci (Gian Luca), Negri (Stefania), "Governing the Global Fight against Pandemics: the WHO, the International Health Regulations, and the Fragmentation of International Law", *New York University journal of international law and politics*, 2021, p. 501.

Burger (Michael), Wentz (Jessica), Horton (Radley), "The Law and Science of Climate Change Attribution", *Columbia journal of environmental law*, 2020, at 57.

Campanelli (Danio), "Solidarity, principle of", *MPEPIL*, March 2011.

Cassella (Sarah), *La nécessité en droit international. De l'état de nécessité aux situations de nécessité*, Leiden, Brill Nijhoff, 2011.

Cassella (Sarah), "Responsabilité(s) de l'Etat pour le risque global lié aux changements climatiques", *Revue générale de droit international public*, 2019/2, at 363.

Cassella (Sarah), "La responsabilité des Etats et des organisations internationales du fait de la pandémie de COVID-19", *Annuaire français de droit international*, 2020, at 51.

Cassella (Sarah), "Les dynamiques de la précaution dans la lutte contre les changements climatiques", *Archives de philosophie du droit*, 2020, at 131.

Cazala (Julien), *Le principe de précaution en droit international*, Louvain-La Neuve, Anthemis, 2006.

Centeno (Miguel A.), Nag (Manish), Patterson (Thayer S.), Shaver (Andrew), Windawi (A. Jason), "The emergence of global systemic risk", *Annual Review of Sociology*, 2015, at 66.

Cima (Elena), Mbengue (Makane Moïse), ""Kind of Green". The U.S. Proposal to Advance Sustainability through Trade Rules and the Future of the WTO", *ESIL Reflections*, 2021.

Clarke (Lisa), *Public-private partnerships and responsibility under international law: a global health perspective*, New York, Routledge, 2014.

Coco (Antonio), De Souza Dias (Talita), "Due Diligence and COVID-19: States' Duties to Prevent and Halt the Coronavirus Outbreak", *EJIL Talk!*, 24 March 2020, <https://www.ejiltalk.org/part-i-due-diligence-and-COVID-19-states-duties-to-prevent-and-halt-the-coronavirus-outbreak/>.

Cornu (Marie), Orsi (Fabienne), Rochfeld (Judith) (eds), *Dictionnaire des biens communs*, Paris, PUF, 2017.

Cournil (Christel), Varison (Leandro), Delmas-Marty (Mireille) (eds), *Les procès climatiques: entre le national et l'international*, Paris, Pedone, 2018.

Creutz (Katja), *State responsibility in the international legal order: a critical appraisal*, Cambridge University Press, 2020.

Crutzen (Paul J.), Stoermer (Eugene F.), "The "Anthropocene"", *International Geosphere-Biosphere Programme Newsletter*, vol. 14 (May 2000), at 17, <http://www.igbp.net>.

Danchin (Peter G.), Farrall (Jeremy), Rana (Shruti), Saunders (Imogen), "The pandemic paradox in international law", *AJIL*, 2020, at 598.

Delmas-Marty (Mireille), *Vers une communauté de valeurs ?*, Paris, Editions du Seuil, 2011.

De Schutter (Olivier), "Public budget analysis for the realisation of economic, social and cultural rights: conceptual framework and practical implementation", at 527, in Young (Katharine G.), *The future of economic and social rights*, Cambridge, CUP, 2019.

Dugard (Jackie), Porter (Bruce), Ikawa (Daniela), Chenwi (Lilian) (eds), *Research handbook on economic, social and cultural rights as human rights*, Cheltenham, Edward Elgar Publishing, 2020.

Dupuy (Pierre-Marie), Viñuales (Jorge E.) (eds), *Harnessing foreign investment to promote environmental protection. Incentives and safeguards*, Cambridge University Press, 2013.

Eccleston-Turner (Mark), McArdle (Scarlett), Upshur (Ross), "Inter-Institutional Relationships in Global Health: Regulating Coordination and Ensuring Accountability", *Global health governance*, 2018, at 83.

Faure (Michael G.), Nollkaemper (André), "International liability as an instrument to prevent and compensate for climate change", *Stanford journal of international law*, 2007, at 123.

Fitzmaurice (Malgosia), "Responsibility and climate change", *German Yearbook of International Law*, 2010, at 89.

Francioni (Francesco), "Sovranità statale e tutela della salute come bene pubblico globale », at 51–66, in Pineschi (Laura) (ed.), *La tutela della salute den diritto internazionale ed europeo tra interessi globali e interessi particolari*, Napoli, Editoriale scientifica, 2017.

Frison-Roche (Marie-Anne), "La responsabilité *Ex-Ante*", *Archives de philosophie du droit*, 2022, at 105.

Ganapathy-Doré (Geetha), Pillai (Mohanan Bhaskaran), (eds), *Global commons. Issues, concerns and strategies*, Los Angeles, Sage, 2020.

Gibney (Mark), Skogly (Sigrun) (eds), *Universal Human Rights and Extraterritorial Obligations*, Philadelphia, University of Pennsylvania Press, 2010.

Giddens (Anthony), "Risk and Responsibility", *The Modern Law Review*, 1999, at 1.

Goldin (Ian), Mariathasan (Mike), *The Butterfly Defect. How globalisation creates systemic risks, and what to do about it*, Princeton University Press, 2014.

Gostin (Lawrence O.), *Global health law*, Cambridge, Harvard University Press, 2014.

Hart (Herbert Lionel Adolphus), *Punishment and Responsibility: Essays in the Philosophy of Law*, Oxford, Clarendon Press, 1968.

Hautereau-Boutonnet (Mathilde), "Quel droit climatique?", *Recueil Dalloz*, 2015, at 2260.

Hautereau-Boutonnet (Mathilde), Truilhé-Marengo (Eve) (eds), *Le procès environnemental: du procès sur l'environnement au procès pour l'environnement. Rapport final de recherche*, Mission de recherche Droit & justice, 2019, <http://www.gip-recherche-justice.fr/publication/le-proces-environnemental-du-proces-sur-lenvironnement-au-proces-pour-lenvironnement/>.

Helbing (Dirk), "Globally Networked Risks and how to Respond", *Nature*, 2013, at 51.

Hestermeyer (Holger P.), "Reality or Aspiration? – Solidarity in International Environmental and World Trade Law" at 45, in *Coexistence, cooperation and solidarity: liber amicorum Rüdiger Wolfrum*, Leiden, Nijhoff, 2012, vol. 2.

Hutter (Bridget M.), *Risk, resilience, inequality and environmental law*, Cheltenham, UK; Northampton, MA, USA, Edward Elgar Publishing, 2017.

Jacobs (Dov), Nollkaemper (André), Schechinger (Jessica N.M.) (eds), *Distribution of responsibilities in international law*, Cambridge University Press, 2015.

Jonas (Hans), *The imperative responsibility. In search for an ethics for the technological age*, The University of Chicago Press, 1984.

Kay (John), King (Mervin), "The Radical Uncertainties of Coronavirus", *Prospect Magazine*, 2020 <www.prospectmagazine.co.uk/magazine/coronavirus-model-uncertainty-kay-king>.

Kerbrat (Yann), Maljean-Dubois (Sandrine), "Les juridictions internationales et le principe de précaution, entre grande prudence et petites audaces", at 929, in *Unity and diversity of international law: essays in honour of Professor Pierre-Marie Dupuy*, Leiden, Martinus Nijhoff Publishers, 2014.

Klabbers (Jan), "Reflections on Role Responsibility: The Responsibility of International Organisations for Failing to Act", *EJIL*, 2018, at 1133.

Klabbers (Jan), "The Normative Gap in International Organisations: the Case of the World Health Organisation", *International Organisations Law Review*, 2019, at 272.

Kleffner (Jann K.), Nollkaemper (André), Plakokefalos (Ilias), Schechinger (Jessica N.M.), (eds), *The practice of shared responsibility in international law*, Cambridge University Press, 2017.

Koroma (Abdul G.), "Solidarity: Evidence of an Emerging International Legal Principle", at 125, in *Coexistence, cooperation and solidarity: liber amicorum Rüdiger Wolfrum*, Leiden, Nijhoff, 2012, vol. 2.

Kreuzer (Leonhard), Krieger (Heige), Peters (Anne) (eds), *Due diligence in the international legal order*, Oxford University Press, 2020.

Lagrange (Evelyne), "L'efficacité des normes internationales concernant la situation des personnes privées dans les ordres juridiques internes", *Collected Courses of The Hague Academy of International Law*, vol. 356, 2012.

Longaretti (Pierre-Yves), "Risques systémiques globaux et risques d'effondrement. Quels éléments d'analyse scientifique, pour quels types de risques?", LIREC *Lettre d'Information sur les Risques et Crises*, Institut national des hautes études de la sécurité et de la justice (INHESJ), 2020, at 1.

Maljean-Dubois (Sandrine), Mehdi (Rostane) (eds), *La société internationale et les grandes pandémies*, Paris, Pedone, 2007.

Maljean-Dubois (Sandrine), "Quel droit international face au changement climatique?", *Recueil Dalloz*, 2015, at 2263.

Maljean-Dubois (Sandrine), "Climate Change Litigation", MPEPIL, June 2018.

Martin (Betsan), Te Aho (Linda), Humphries-Kil (Maria) (eds), *Responsability. Law and governance for living well with the Earth*, New York, Routledge, 2019.

Mbengue (Makane Moise), *Essai sur une théorie du risque en droit international public. L'anticipation du risque environnemental et sanitaire*, Paris, Pedone, 2009.

Mbengue (Makane Moise), Sindico (Francesco) (eds), *Comparative climate change litigation: beyond the usual suspects*, Cham, Springer Nature, 2021.

Minnerop (Petra), "Climate Protection Agreements", MPEPIL, March 2018.

Morin (Edgar), "Au-delà du réductionnisme et du holisme: la complexité du global", at 441, in Wieviorka (Michel), Lévi-Strauss (Laurent), Lieppe (Gwenaëlle) (eds), *Penser global. Internationalisation et globalisation des sciences humaines et sociales*, Maison des Sciences de l'Homme, 2015.

Murase (Shinya), Zhou (Suzanna) (eds), *Epidemics and international law*, Leiden, Brill Nijhoff, 2021.

Negri (Stefania), *Salute pubblica, sicurezza e diritti umani nel diritto internazionale*, Torino, G. Giappichelli Editore, 2018.

Negri (Stefania) (ed.), *Environmental health in international and EU law. Current challenges and legal responses*, Torino, G. Giappichelli Editore, 2020.

Nijman (Janne E.), Nollkaemper (André), *New Perspectives on the Divide between National and International Law*, Oxford University Press, 2007.

Nollkaemper (André), "Three Conceptions of the Integration Principle in International Environmental Law", at 24 in Lenschow (Andrea) (ed.), *Environmental Policy Integration. Greening Sectoral Policies in Europe*, London, Routledge, 2001.

Nollkaemper (André), "Internationally Wrongful Acts in Domestic Courts", AJIL, 2007, at 760.

Nollkaemper, (André), *National Courts and the International Rule of Law*, Oxford University Press, 2011.

Nollkaemper (André), "International Adjudication of Global Public Goods: The Intersection of Substance and Procedure", EJIL, 2012, at 769.

Nollkaemper (André), "Responsibility", at 764, in D'Aspremont (Jean), Singh (Sahib) (eds), *Concepts for International Law: Contributions to Disciplinary Thought*, Cheltenham, Edward Elgar Publishing, 2019.

Paparinskis (Martins), "COVID-19 claims and the law of international responsibility", *Journal of international Humanitarian Legal Studies*, 2020, at 311.

Paparinskis (Martins), "The once and future law of State responsibility", AJIL, 2020, at 618.

Pavoni (Riccardo), "Mutual Supportiveness as a Principle of Interpretation and Law-Making: a Watershed for the "WTO-and-Competing-Regimes" Debate?", EJIL, 2010, at 649.

Petersmann (Ernst Ulrich), *Multilevel constitutionalism for multilevel governance of public goods: methodology problems in international law*, Oxford, Hart Publishing, 2017.

Pisillo Mazzeschi (Riccardo), "Responsabilité de l'État pour violation des obligations positives relatives aux droits de l'Homme", *Collected Courses of The Hague Academy of International Law*, vol. 333, 2008.

Quirico (Ottavio), "Systemic integration between climate change and human rights in international law?", *Netherlands quarterly of human rights*, 2017, at 31.

Rajamani (Lavanya), "Innovation and experimentation in the international climate change regime", *Collected Courses of the Hague Academy of International Law*, vol. 404, 2020.

Rayfuse (Rosemary Gail), Scott (Shirley V.) (eds), *International law in the era of climate change*, Cheltenham; Northampton, Edward Elgar, 2012.

Ricoeur (Paul), "Postface", at 251, in Lenoir (Frédéric) (ed.), *Le temps de la responsabilité. Entretiens sur l'éthique*, Paris, Fayard, 1991.

Ruppel (Oliver Christian), Roschmann (Christian), Ruppel-Schlichting (Katharina) (eds), *Climate Change: International Law and Global Governance, Volume I: Legal Responses and Global Responsibility*, Baden Baden, Nomos, 2013.

Ryngaert (Cedric), "Territory in the Law of Jurisdiction: Imagining Alternatives", *Netherlands Yearbook of International Law*, 2017, at 60.

Samson (Mélanie), "L'Organisation mondiale du commerce: un forum approprié pour la protection de la santé publique?", in Kohen (Marcelo), Bentolila (Dolores) (eds), *Mélanges en l'honneur du professeur Jean-Michel Jacquet: le droit des rapports internationaux économiques et privés*, Paris, LexisNexis, 2013.

Sands (Philip), Peel (Jaqueline), Fabra Aguilar (Adriana), Mckenzie (Ruth), *Principles of international environmental law*, Cambridge University Press, 2018.

Schröder (Meinhard), "Precautionary approach/principle", *MPEPIL*, March 2014.

SFDI, *La responsabilité de protéger*, Paris, Pedone, 2008.

SFDI, *Le standard de* due diligence *et la responsabilité internationale. Journée d'études franco-italienne du Mans*, Paris, Pedone, 2018.

Soltau (Friedrich), "Common concern of Humankind", at 202, in Gray (Kevin R.), Tarasofsky (Richard), Carlarne (Cinnamon) (eds), *The Oxford handbook of international climate change law*, OUP, 2016.

Stoll (Peter-Tobias), "The Climate as a Global Common", at 131, in Farber (Daniel A.), Peeters (Marjan) (eds), *Climate Change Law, vol. 1, Elgar Encyclopedia of Environmental Law*, Cheltenham; Northampton, Edward Elgar Publishing, 2016.

Sucharitkul (Sompong), "State Responsibility and International Liability Under International Law", *Loyola of Los Angeles International & Comparative Law Journal*, 1996, at 821.

Supiot (Alain), Delmas-Marty (Mireille) (eds), *Prendre la responsabilité au sérieux*, Paris, PUF, 2015.

Supiot (Alain) (ed.), *Face à l'irresponsabilité: la dynamique de la solidarité*, Paris, Collège de France, 2018.

Thibierge (Catherine), "Avenir de la responsabilité, responsabilité de l'avenir", *Recueil Dalloz*, 2004, at 577.

Tirole (Jean), "Country Solidarity in Sovereign Crises", *The American Economic Review*, 2015, at 2333.

Titi (Catharine) (ed.), *Droits de l'homme et droit international économique*, Bruxelles, Bruylant, 2019.

Torre-Schaub (Marta), "Justice climatique: vers quelles responsabilités allons-nous?", *Revue juridique de l'environnement*, 2019, at 129.

Trachtman (Joel P.), *The economic structure of international law*, Cambridge, Harvard University Press, 2008.

Vadi (Valentina), "Beyond known worlds: climate change governance by arbitral tribunals?", *Vanderbilt Journal of Transnational Law*, 2015, at 1329.

Verhoeven (Joe), "Considérations sur ce qui est commun", *Collected Courses of the Hague Academy of International Law*, vol. 334, 2002.

Villey (Michel), "Esquisse historique sur le mot responsible", *Archives de philosophie du droit*, 1977, at 45.

Viñuales (Jorge E.), *Foreign investment and the environment in international law*, Cambridge University Press, 2012.

Voigt (Christina), "State Responsibility for Climate Change Damages", *Nordic Journal of International Law*, 2008, at 1.

Villarreal (Pedro A.), Bogdandy (Armin von), "International law on pandemic response: a first stocktaking in light of the Coronavirus crisis", *MPIL Research Paper Series* No. 2020–07.

Wewerinke-Singh (Margaretha), Hinge Salili (Diana), "Between negotiations and litigation: Vanuatu's perspective on loss and damage from climate change", *Climate policy*, 2019, <https://doi.org/10.1080/14693062.2019.1623166>Young (Margaret A.), *Regime interaction in international law*, Cambridge University Press, 2012.

Zarka (Yves Charles), "Considérations philosophiques sur le principe de precaution", *Revue de métaphysique et de morale*, 2012, at 483.

Table of Cases

1 International Courts and Tribunals, Treaty Bodies

African Commission on Human and People's Rights

Social and Economic Rights Centre (*SERAC*) *and Centre for Economic and Social Rights* (*CESR*) *v. Nigeria*, decision of 27 October 2001

Arbitral Tribunals

Trail smelter case (*United States, Canada*), award, 16 April 1938 and 11 March 1941

S.D. Myers, Inc. v. Government of Canada, award, 13 November 2000

LG & E Energy Corp. and others v Argentina, decision on Liability, 3 October 2006, no ARB/02/1

Philip Morris Brands SARL, Philip Morris Products SA v Uruguay, award, 8 July 2016, no ARB/10/7

Committee on the Rights of the Child

Sacchi et al. v. Argentina et al., decisions adopted on 8 October 2021

Court of Justice of the European Union

ECJ, *Armando Ferrão Carvalho and Others v. The European Parliament and the Council*, judgment, 25 March 2021

European Court of Human Rights

Grand Chamber, *Guerra and others v. Italy*, 19 February 1998, application no 14967/89

Budayeva and Others v. Russia, 20 March 2008, applications nos 15339/02, 21166/02, 20058/02, 11673/02 and 15343/02

Tătar v. Romania, 27 January 2009, application no 67021/01

Di Sarno and others v. Italy, 10 January 2012, application no. 30765/08

Stichting mothers of Srebrenica and others v. The Netherlands, 11 June 2013, application no 65542/12

Al-Dulimi and Montana Management Inc. v. Switzerland, 21 June 2016, application no 5809/08

Le Mailloux v. France, 5 November 2020, application no 18108/20

Humane Being v. the United Kingdom, 13 December 2022, application no no. 36959/22

Human Rights Committee

Munaf v. Romania, 21 August 2009

Daniel Billy and others v. Australia (*Torres Strait Islanders Petition*), views adopted by the Committee under article 5 (4) of the Optional Protocol, concerning communication no. 3624/2019

Inter-American Commission on Human Rights

Petition to the Inter-American Commission on Human Rights Seeking Relief from Violations of the Rights of Arctic Athabaskan Peoples Resulting from Rapid Arctic Warming and Melting Caused by Emissions of Black Carbon by Canada, filed on the 23 April 2013

Inter-American Court of Human Rights

Velasquez Rodriguez v. Honduras, judgment, 29 July 1988

A Request for an Advisory Opinion from the Inter-American Court of Human Rights Concerning the Interpretation of Article 1(1), 4(1) and 5(1) of the American Convention on Human Rights), advisory opinion, 15 November 2017

Request for an advisory opinion on the Climate Emergency and Human Rights submitted to the Inter-American Court of Human Rights by the Republic of Colombia and the Republic of Chile, 9 January 2023

International Court of Justice

Legality of the Threat or Use of Nuclear Weapons, advisory opinion, 8 July 1996

Gabčíkovo-Nagymaros Project (*Hungary/Slovakia*), judgment, 25 September 1997

Pulp Mills on the River Uruguay (*Argentina v. Uruguay*), judgment, 20 April 2010

Certain Activities Carried Out by Nicaragua in the Border Area (*Costa Rica v. Nicaragua*) and *Construction of a Road in Costa Rica along the San Juan River* (*Nicaragua v. Costa Rica*), judgment, 16 December 2015

Certain Activities Carried Out by Nicaragua in the Border Area (*Costa Rica v. Nicaragua*), judgment, 2 February 2018

Obligations of States in respect of Climate Change, request for an advisory opinion, 12 April 2023

International Tribunal for the Law of the Sea

Responsibilities and obligations of States sponsoring persons and entities with respect to activities in the Area (*Request for Advisory Opinion submitted to the Seabed Disputes Chamber*), advisory opinion, 1 February 2011

Request for an Advisory Opinion submitted by the Commission of Small Island States on Climate Change and International Law, 12 December 2022

Permanent Court of Arbitration

Iron Rhine Arbitration (*Belgium/Netherlands*), award, 24 May 2005
The South China Sea Arbitration (*The Republic of Philippines v. The People's Republic of China*), award, 12 July 2016

WTO Dispute Settlement Body

Appellate Body, *European Communities—Measures Affecting Asbestos and Products Containing Asbestos*, 12 March 2001, WT/DS135/AB/R
Appellate Body, *Brazil—Measures Affecting Imports of Retreaded Tyres*, 3 December 2007, WT/DS332/AB/R

2 Domestic Courts

The following decisions may be found – in most cases with an English translation – in two databases: for climate litigation, <http://climatecasechart.com/>; for litigation related to the COVID-19 pandemic, <https://www.COVID19litigation.org/about>.

Belgium

Brussels Court of First Instance, *VZW Klimaatzaak v. Kingdom of Belgium & Others*, 17 June 2021

Brazil

Supreme Court, *PSB et al v Brazil* (*on Climate Fund*), 1 July 2022

Colombia

Supreme Court of Colombia, *Future Generations v. Ministry of the Environment and Others*, 5 April 2018

Czech Republic

Prague Municipal Court, judgment no. 14A 101/2021, 15 June 2022

France

Council of State, *Commune de Grande-Synthe v. France*, 19 November 2020
Administrative Court of Paris, *Notre Affaire à Tous and Others v. France*, 3 February 2021
Administrative Court of Paris, *Notre Affaire à Tous and Others v. France*, 14 October 2021
Council of State, *Mme M.B.*, 28 June 2022, no 2012679/6-3

Germany

Federal Constitutional Court, *Neubauer, et al. v. Germany*, 24 March 2021

Guatemala

Constitutional Court, 28 January 2021, Expediente 2758–2020

Mexico

Sixth District Court of the State of Sinaloa, 10 May 2021, Case no. 208/2020-3B

Eleventh Collegiate Court of the First Circuit in Administrative Matters, *Greenpeace v. Instituto Nacional de Ecología y Cambio Climático and Others*, 21 September 2021

Nepal

Supreme Court of Nepal, *Shrestha v. Office of the Prime Minister et al.*, 25 December 2018

New Zealand

High Court of New Zealand, *Thomson v. Minister for Climate Change Issues*, 2 November 2017

Pakistan

Lahore High Court, *Leghari v. Federation of Pakistan*, 25 January 2018

Paraguay

Civil and Commercial Court of Appeals of Asunción, Fifth Chamber, *Ministry of Public Health and Social Welfare s/Ampa*, 15 June 2021

South Africa

High Court, *EarthLife Africa Johannesburg v. Minister of Environmental Affairs and Others*, 6 March 2017

The Netherlands

Supreme Court, *Nuhanovic v. the Dutch State*, Case no 12/03324, 6 September 2013

Hague Appeals Court, *Stichting Mothers of Srebrenica et al. v. The Netherlands*, Case no C/09/295247, 16 July 2014

The Hague District Court, *Urgenda Foundation v. State of the Netherlands*, 24 June 2015

The Hague Court of Appeals, *Urgenda Foundation v. State of the Netherlands*, 9 October 2018

The Hague District Court, *Milieudefensie et al. v. Royal Dutch Shell plc.*, 26 May 2021

United Kingdom

High Court of Justice, *R (oao Friends of the Earth) v. Secretary of State for Business Energy and Industrial Strategy*, 18 July 2022

United States of America

United States Supreme Court, *Massachusetts et al. v. Environmental protection agency et al.* (*Massachusetts v. EPA*), 2 April 2007

Juliana v. United States, no 18–36082, 9th Cir., 17 January 2020

Index

www.ingramcontent.com/pod-product-compliance
Lightning Source LLC
Chambersburg PA
CBHW071225230926
51849CB00001B/31
9789004538696